Mark Nielson

S0-AXY-876

The Twin

Mark Nielson

The Twin

Donald Richardson

WestBow
PRESS
A DIVISION OF THOMAS NELSON

Copyright © 2013 Donald Richardson.

Cover created by Todd & Surisa

All rights reserved. No part of this book may be used or reproduced by any means, graphic, electronic, or mechanical, including photocopying, recording, taping or by any information storage retrieval system without the written permission of the publisher except in the case of brief quotations embodied in critical articles and reviews.

WestBow Press books may be ordered through booksellers or by contacting:

WestBow Press
A Division of Thomas Nelson
1663 Liberty Drive
Bloomington, IN 47403
www.westbowpress.com
1 (866) 928-1240

Because of the dynamic nature of the Internet, any web addresses or links contained in this book may have changed since publication and may no longer be valid. The views expressed in this work are solely those of the author and do not necessarily reflect the views of the publisher, and the publisher hereby disclaims any responsibility for them.

Bible versions: King James & RSV

Any people depicted in stock imagery provided by Thinkstock are models, and such images are being used for illustrative purposes only. Certain stock imagery © Thinkstock.

ISBN: 978-1-4908-2100-9 (sc)
ISBN: 978-1-4908-2099-6 (e)

Library of Congress Control Number: 2013923445

Printed in the United States of America.

WestBow Press rev. date: 01/09/13

Dedicated to

Brent, Drew, Astrid, Jesse, Troy, Max, Zoe, and Chloe

Preface

A T FIRST GLANCE this book appears to be another attempt to arrange and paraphrase Gospel accounts for a popular readership, which at one level it certainly is. That, however, is not its primary task. What I mean it to be is an inquiry into meaning. The Apostle Thomas's is the viewpoint of the narrative. He is the kid in the classroom who always has his hand up. He has to get things right, has to have them make sense, has to know when to take things literally and when to take them figuratively. He has to know where reason leaves off and faith begins and where clarity leaves off and we have to admit to mystery.

I lived my life as a university professor, and I always loved the Thomases that came along. They were the ones that had to know. It was never enough for them to write down information for later recall or read about the thoughts of others; they pressed to know where the thoughts were coming from, what assumptions underlay them, and what implications logically followed. These bright lights' intellectual digestive systems were essentially bovine: they swallowed their cerebral fodder and ruminated on it, then coughed it up to chew on it some more, and then repeated the process another time or two. They drifted into my office and dropped by the house. They were not shy about admitting their ignorance nor shocked when I admitted mine.

The Thomas of these pages is my take on the Thomas of the Gospels, but he is also, I suspect, an amalgam of all the other Thomases I have known over the years—as well as myself. He was first and foremost a man of faith. There is every indication that, when Jesus called him, he (no less than Peter, Andrew, John, James, Philip and Nathanael, whom he called a week or so earlier) turned away from his routine life and fell in immediately behind him. The sway Jesus had over him was absolute.

But his faith was in no way at odds with his reason. His struggle was to coordinate the former with the latter, not choose the one or the other. Perhaps more conspicuously than his fellows, he was the prototypical Christian thinker. And, who knows, maybe that is why his fellows nicknamed him the Twin and others later have tagged him Doubting Thomas.

I make Levi Matthew, former publican and future evangelist, Thomas's ideological sidekick, the person with whom he is forever comparing notes and whose opinions he most values, for Matthew seems to be the disciple best versed in the Old Testament Scriptures. They talk about what Jesus says and does, trying between them to understand where He is coming from and where He is going and what are at the cores of some of the terms He uses: *kingdom, save, born again, eternal life,* and *faith.*

My working premise is that Thomas' contemporaries were looking for a Christ on the order of a super David who would rescue them from enemies current and future and establish a new Kingdom of God headquartered at Jerusalem with Him as their king into indefinite time to come. But Thomas and Matthew, among others, begin to wonder if maybe Jesus' real kingdom is not the kingdom his contemporaries take it to be and, in the same vein, if maybe He himself is someone more than the long-awaited new David whose coronation is imminent.

The scene of the disciples' final departure to Jerusalem gives us a good indication of what most of His followers were probably expecting even that late in the game. The issue comes up as to who's going to be what when his kingdom comes; and John and James, key disciples, and their mother are in the thick of it. Judas clearly expects to be Secretary of Treasury.

Words do not always mean, Thomas and Matthew early on begin to realize, what people always take them to mean. Who or what, they wonder, is the Savior going to save them from? The Romans, their own officious rulers? Such might be one's first assumption, but maybe Jesus' point of reference is far afield from those options. What does He mean when he tells Nicodemus he must be born again? Faith, Jesus insists, is the elusive key to inclusion in His kingdom. How does one come by it and how does one know he has it? Who is Jesus really? The questions abound.

And so this book is about meaning: what people seem to think Jesus meant and what he might have really meant instead. There is a lot of speculation in the dialogues between Thomas and Matthew. And there are points where both are stumped, when neither one can say anything with reasonable certainty.

My narrative material is from the four Gospels, and my paraphrasing of it is consistent with the evangelists' accounts. For some aspects of the political climate, particularly with regard to the Zealots and the Sicarii, I go to Josephus' *The Jewish Wars*. And, yes, I do try to flesh out the images of certain people who knew Jesus: Thomas in particular and also Matthew, Simon the Zealot, and Judas Iscariot (and to a lesser extent Peter, John, Nathanael, and Philip). In so doing I draw a lot on inferences from the Gospels. But, apart from things Jesus actually said, the dialogue is mostly mine; it's the way I imagine these disciples' conversations might have gone. The thoughts are thoughts that had to have crossed their minds. And I do own to having read a quite a bit of Plato and maybe should have titled this book *The Dialogues of Thomas*.

There is, I should point out, a real *Gospel of Thomas*. It is not in the New Testament canon but it is among the *Dead Sea Scrolls*, and there is one snippet from that short manuscript I include in mine. This is the point at which Jesus asks select disciples whom they would compare Him to. And, when He asks Thomas, he answers, "Nobody. You are like no one or nothing I've ever known. To me, I must confess, you are still an utter mystery." The passage fits.

Distinctions

T HEY'VE TAKEN TO calling him the Twin, and he doesn't know why. There's seldom any sense, he realizes, about the tags they put on a fellow. Somebody misunderstands what your real name is and takes a stab at what he thinks he heard someone call you and gets it totally wrong and you have a brand new moniker. Or maybe somebody calls you something out of the blue because he thinks it's funny and, lo and behold, the silly thing sticks. There's no accounting for it. Now who ever got it into his head he was somebody's twin? That's what he'd like to know. His poor mother's certainly going to have the shock of her life when she hears of this.

Some of the new men don't even seem to know he has another name. It's the Twin this and the Twin that, all straight-faced and natural, just as though they know lots of guys named the Twin and he's just the latest of them. Does he exude something that says twin to them? Do they see something he doesn't? Is he in some sense two of anybody? Call him what they may—it really doesn't matter. The Twin, though. Weird thing to call a man.

The Master himself still calls him Thomas, so there's hope. If he keeps doing it, maybe the others will pick up on it and get it right.

After this morning's wrangle there are probably a lot more things they're calling him behind his back, so the Twin might not be the worst thing in the world. He's clearly not their favorite yoke fellow right now. They avoided his eyes then as now, and their voices involuntarily jumped a note and seemed to crackle when they snapped back at him. All that because he referred to Jesus' turning water into wine as an act of magic, which it clearly was.

"A miracle!" the taller of the two urbanites shot back at him. Philip.

"Magic is hocus pocus," his buddy came in, an edge in his voice too. "What we're talking about is a miracle, my good sir, an honest to goodness miracle!"

Without intending to, he'd somehow shaken a red blanket in the faces of a small bull herd already skittish about his even being allowed in the holding pen. You'd have thought he'd just blurted out a lewd insult against their mothers and grandmothers and all the granddames before them.

"All right, miracle if you will. I didn't intend to demean the act," he quickly recovered. "Nothing to get in a huff about. We'll go with your label. Fine with me. This incident happened down in Cana, you say?"

They said it did.

"And you were there, and you saw it with your own eyes?"

"With our own eyes we saw the new wine served and with our own ears heard what the chief guests were saying about it, yes," confirmed Philip. "And Nathanael here has known one of the wine-pourers since boyhood. He comes from down that way, you know. They told him exactly, step by step, where the new wine came from."

He then went on to recite again the narrative he'd already, in step by step detail, told Thomas not ten minutes earlier, albeit a longer, slower version. With pronounced whole-body gestures and overdone vocal impersonations of each player, he got his hands, head, arms, and torso all into the act, and, with no want of excitement, took on the persona of everybody present when the supposed supernatural act took place.

Nathanael stood beside his fellow metropolitan, nodding assent to everything his comrade said; the four fishermen, also present, pressed in close but said nothing, although it was clear from their facial expressions that they heartily approved the narration and were not a little irked that it had to be repeated.

Philip had obviously told the story a number of times now, and they had all enjoyed it like a rare banquet when he did. And for good reason: it was a great little story.

Thomas listened with patience, although not with the raised

eyebrows and gasps of amazement the performer was apparently expecting. He'd originally heard the narrative from rumormongers and already both a short and expanded version from Philip, and so there was little by way of suspense or surprise to react to this time around. But, though not especially expressive, he was sufficiently well mannered to hear the man out.

Politeness, however, was not the response Philip was going for. Out of probably no more than exasperation, Thomas now suspects, the actor upped his histrionics; and, still not getting anticipated reaction, totally overplayed the finale. Leaning in so close to him that their noses were no more than span apart, Philip snapped, accusingly and perhaps louder than he intended, "What? Do you not believe in miracles?"

Thomas was slow to answer. He wanted no quarrels with his new companions, but at the same time he did have to be true to himself. He felt the gaze of all six men upon him

"I believe in the possibility of miracles, yes," he finally answered thoughtfully. "Whoever put this world together in the first place must certainly have the prerogative of intruding into His own natural order at any given time to tweak it however He wants. Yes, that premise seems entirely logical. And I suspect He actually does indulge in minor touchups every once in a rare while. By all means put me down as a true believer in miracles, but. .."

"But . . .?"

"But I do not think that in any given case, no matter how great the aberration may seem to be, we should be crying, 'Eureka, a miracle!' before first exhausting all other possible explanations. If miracles become common-day events, they would no longer be miracles, now would they? A lot of things in this world seem miraculous but upon closer examination do not strictly qualify as such."

"How about Moses' turning his staff into a serpent?" came in the big fisherman. "Would you call that a miracle?"

Yes, he agreed, he thought he would.

"And his dividing the Red Sea?"

"Yes, that too in all likelihood would qualify as a miracle."

"Joshua's bringing down the walls of Jericho?"

Thomas pondered this one, then shook his head slowly. "That I don't know," he finally said. "Could have happened because of something in the walls' compositions. There've been incidents, I've been told, of solid bridges suddenly collapsing when companies of soldiers have marched across them. If so, could not the city walls have been shaken loose by much the same phenomenon?"

"What about David's killing of Goliath? Do you consider that a miracle?"

"What I think is that the young fellow was one whale of shot. A miracle? No, probably not. Not unless you call his killing a lion just prior to that with the very same slingshot a miracle. Not unless you call Absalom's getting his hair caught in the branches of a tree a miracle. Maybe my definition of a miracle is too restrictive. I would say something is a miracle only if it involves some clear momentary breach in the natural order of things. Otherwise I would call such things as the fall of the walls of Jericho and David's slaying Goliath instances of divine providence. God may have guided the action in such cases though not by suspending the natural order but rather by simply invoking it."

None of the men seemed to see where he was going. They exchanged looks, each screwing up his face in the process of appearing thoughtful—overly much so, Thomas thought. But, after all, they'd just come off a gesture-loaded narrative and were still in that mode. He understood, he really did. They simply weren't all that much into abstract thinking. Not everybody was.

"Forget about Goliath. What we have here is someone's changing water into wine," Philip said

"Ah, to the case in point," he said. "I regret I was not there to see that. The urns that they filled with water, I think you said, were stone. Is that correct?"

"Yes, they were of stone."

"Well, let me tell you what the skeptic might say, not that I own to being a skeptic myself, you understand. Our skeptic will point out that stone is porous, so there had to have been some wine residue in the pores and most likely a splash or so at the bottom of each vat, sufficient to give the water a wine bouquet as well as flavor. And there could have been a whole lot more wine in some of the wedding guests themselves than the pourers realized. Just a possibility, mind you. So the water in question was probably diluted with at least a little bit of the real stuff. If you give diluted wine to people who've been imbibing for the better part of an afternoon, some are bound to interpret the different taste as maybe a different wine. And some might attribute that difference to the new wine's being superior. A little farfetched, but I think that's roughly what you'd be getting from a true skeptic."

"But what about you?"

"I don't know. I wasn't there. If I were, I'd probably be telling people the same story you've just told me. As it is, right now I'd have to say I do lean in that direction. Most of you did, however, get the account second or thirdhand, did you not?"

This clearly upset Philip. "A miracle," he continued to insist, "pure and simple."

"Probably," Thomas conceded, "but miracle is not always the only explanation. That's all I'm saying. If it was indeed a miracle, don't you wonder why he did it, why he chose that particular thing? Was it so crucial that the wedding guests have second, third and fourth goblets of wine?"

"Maybe for the same reason Moses was given his enchanted staff. It got people's attention."

"But he's done other miracles too," the younger of the sons of Zebedee then pointed out. "There are the healings. He's lifted nameless cripples to their feet, cleansed lepers, made the wounded whole."

Thomas had heard these stories too, at least some of them. One involved a relative of the big fisherman Peter once called Simon—his own mother, it seemed. She was apparently, according those around her, on her deathbed, and the Master simply by touching her on her forehead had broken her fever in an instant. *Maybe it was only his mother-in-law.* At any rate, before you knew it, she was up and around whipping up a veritable banquet for the whole houseful of people who had shown up to see the poor woman take her final breath. Some stayed to eat the fine meal; others rushed out and dragged back every invalid and cripple from as far away as Chorazin and Bethsaida.

"I've heard," he told them. "Miracles of mercy. In some ways these make more sense to me. More consistent with his character."

"Which is?"

"He empathizes with people," Thomas said, eyeing those about for some gesture of concurrence. "The matter here, however, is whether or not in his empathy the Master circumvented the laws of the natural order or simply employed them."

"We were all there!" shouted Philip, apparently taking Thomas's remark as a denial of everything they've told him up till now.

"One moment the woman is staring death straight in the eye, and the next she's up cooking," then said Peter emphatically, his voice, agitated, as big as he was. "Then half that night a stream of sick and invalid souls showed up at the doorstep to be healed. And they were."

"I do believe you," said Thomas, "but . . .."

"But nothing. I'm telling you I saw it with my own eyes! His presence, his proximity to those poor sick people. He healed them. Instantly, on the spot."

"I said I believe you. But I've heard divine healing stories all my life and in some instances have wondered if perhaps some element of coincidence might have been involved. That's all. In the natural order of things people's fevers are often of a sudden cut. Burning hot one moment, cool as a winter's snow the next. A magic potion or a prayer perhaps gets the credit. Or maybe someone who just happens to be standing there."

"Yes, but the fever always takes its toll. The person is weak for days, has to sleep it off. Has no stamina, no strength. But, I tell you, this woman was chockful of strength, as spry as a sheep sprung from the stable at springtime. Nobody in that room had more sheer energy than she did."

"And I've no reason to dispute that."

"What about our big haul of fish?" James then popped up. "There we were, up half the night in all the best spots and not a thing. Not so much as a fingerling. Comes dawn, and still not a single fish for all our effort."

"Not one fish," Peter confirmed.

"And we were almost at shore's edge when he told us to cast our nets on the other side of our boats. Appeared there all of a sudden and told us how we should fish. So, mostly to humor him, we went out just beyond the drop-off and threw our nets back in, and within the minute, mind you, we began to feel the heft of fish in them—within the minute, I tell you."

"Yes, within the minute!"

"And in we pulled them, and there, would you believe it, were more fish than I think were ever drawn from those waters. In no time at all we were able to fill both boats so full that the water was splashing over the gunwales. Biggest haul at one time we ever had. So that's another one for you."

"This was just as the sun was rising?" Thomas asked.

"That was exactly the time."

"Could it not be then that the fish were schooling closer to the surface, which I understand they often do early on, and that maybe he might just have noticed the sun reflecting off their scales and so knew just where to send you? I suggest that only as an alternate explanation. Could have been a miracle or could have been good observation and analysis. Personally I have no quarrel with either explanation."

"But you seem to be questioning what we just told you."

"I'm sorry. I did not mean to," Thomas apologized to him. "I'm only talking theoretically. About our tendency to embrace unwarranted conclusions in general, not about particular cases. I'm just leery about jumping to cause and effect conclusions too conveniently and too quickly."

"You sound like a theologian," said Philip.

"Don't you believe anything?" Nathanael then asked him. He was conspicuously uncomfortable. So also were the others. Emotions were surfacing, the voices getting louder. "You've been rubbing shoulders with too many Greeks."

"I've bumped into a couple Greeks or so over the years maybe, but please do not mark me the skeptic," said Thomas, a note of apology in his voice. "I'm not. I'm just a man trying to make sense out of something of which I understand so very little. Distinctions must be made between hearsay and truth, between illusion and reality. The extent to which our confidence in someone derives from hearsay and illusion is the extent to which we might later lose that confidence, if and when the shaky underpinnings are yanked away."

"I don't know what you mean."

"Tell me, did you not believe Jesus to be the promised Christ of God before any of these miracles took place?"

Both Nathanael and John quickly said they did, then the others.

"And was that not primarily because of his demeanor and manner of speaking? His gentle air of authority, the blatant wisdom of his words? He said, 'Follow me,' and you followed him. Right? No hesitation. Because, though he spoke softly, you picked up an arresting quality in his voice? He sounded like the Christ you always imagined?"

They conceded that what he said was true.

"And there was a wisdom and insight in his words you'd never ever before in your lives encountered. His utterances were not like the babble of our theologians. He was a breath of fresh air. Was that not your experience too?"

"Yes."

"So you don't think he might be the one?" Peter asked him.

Thomas nodded. "On the contrary, I do think he is. I certainly hope he is."

"What more do you want?"

"I want him to say it. With my own two ears I want to hear him declare it."

"How else can he do what he does except that God be with him?"

"Ah, back to the miracles. God was with Moses, Elijah, Elisha, and Daniel. You said so yourselves. They also performed supernatural acts, but none of them was the Christ. They did what they could to save Israel, although their efforts were, as I recall, all short-lived. The Christ, as I take the prophecies, is supposed to be the savior forever and ever."

"Well?"

"I would just like to hear him say it himself, which by your question, he apparently has not yet in so many words so far said. Am I right in that inference?"

"Do you not find all that we told you unbelievably amazing?" Nathanael pursued.

"Yes," Thomas answered him, "I do. And we'll no doubt see a time, maybe right soon, when some people will even demand yet more miracles for confirmation. But not us I hope. All he has to do is say he's the Christ, just tell us right out."

"And when he does?"

"Then there'll be no holding me down," he told them. "To the death then will I follow him if he requires that of me."

"And I too," said Peter, "although I'm good now."

"The Baptizer said Jesus was the Christ," then said John.

"Did you hear him with your own ears, or was that something secondhand too?"

"I heard him with my own ears. So did Andrew."

Andrew, Peter's brother, assented to this with a vigorous nodding of his head.

"What? Is it somehow a heresy that I want to hear it from him?" Thomas asked as the men began to break up, each to go his own way. "Is it wrong that I want to hear him say it himself?"

His fellow disciples were by then five or six paces away and were going into Capernaum, whereas he was making his exit from the city. None of them answered him. Whether this was because he spoke too softly and they didn't hear him or because they were upset by the tenor of their conversation and were making a statement by just walking away—that he did not then know.

And he still doesn't.

Did one of them, he wonders, maybe start that Twin thing on

purpose because for some reason they thought he was cozy with the Greeks? He said he might have rubbed shoulders with a few in his time, which was true, although he cannot at the moment think of a single Greek he'd ever had a serious conversation with. He was bound to have said something to one of them at one time or another. Greek traders occasionally frequented the agora in Capernaum, and he must have said something by way of pleasantry to some of them, though nothing of consequence. He told his fellow disciples the truth. They could take it any way they wanted to. As though a Galilean didn't have a mind of his own and had to get his cues from elsewhere to think something through!

He's now worked himself up to a pitch all over again. "Reasonableness is not the exclusive property of people far away and centuries removed," he says sharply aloud to himself. "These guys seem to think rationality is somehow the singular province of the Greeks. Not so! Thinking is every bit as much ours as it is the Greeks'."

Then he smiles self-consciously and laughs aloud over his brief soliloquy. Maybe he is two people after all, his own twin: two selves, theorist and critic, fixed in tradition but explorer of new ground. His argument has not been so much with others as with himself. The Twin, however he came by the name, ironically might just fit him.

Incident at Nazareth

A WEEK HAS NOW taken the edge off tempers. Maybe time has been Thomas's friend by allowing his new kindred spirits to ponder the distinctions he was trying to make and has brought them to his conclusions or, more likely, it has enshrouded the whole matter in a cloud so that it's become no more than a blur.

On his own part he has meticulously eschewed abstract thought as the stuff of friendly chitchat. It has been a conscious effort, but he has been holding his tongue of late and nodded his head so much it seems to be on a hinge rather than a pivot. The affable side of his twindom has, out of necessity, taken charge. Now that their ranks have risen to nine, it is critical, he's decided, that petty distinctions give way to ponderous truths.

All buddy now and no longer on guard, he walks briskly between the two urbanites, all heading west and south to Nazareth, Jesus' hometown. Jesus sets the pace, with the four fishermen directly behind him and the three of them next and then the two new men bringing up the rear

"There's one miracle we didn't get to talk about," says Philip.

This gives Thomas an uncomfortable moment. *Easy, boy, easy,* he tells himself. "And which one was that?" he asks out loud, trying to sound casual.

"The big one. I don't know how we could have missed it."

"Seems as though we hit them all."

"Got in the one about the fish," says Nathanael, the hint of a smile at the corners of his lips, "but missed the one about the fishermen. You probably wouldn't have noticed, but our two brother combos have all become noticeably more civilized than they used to be. Not nearly as loud as we'd been accustomed to their being."

"A happy phenomenon you'd probably call it, not having been around them so much," adds Philip. "We call it an out-and-out miracle"

"Still louder than normal people, still shouting as though they have to be heard above the roar of a storm at sea, but discernibly quieter than we've ever known them to be," Philip assures him.

"Word is that folk up in Damascus have quit complaining about them."

"Used to be that they hooted it up like a pack of hyenas every time they came in with a big catch and growled like a pride of lions every time they didn't. Didn't matter who was within earshot. Turned the air purple with their cussing."

"But all of a sudden now the mothers of Capernaum don't have to clamp their hands over their children's ears any more when they go down to the shore."

"Good fellows now I'd have to say. No raucous carryings-on, no cantankerous hairsplitting scuffles with them either. Folk used to call the Bar-Zebedee brothers 'the Sons of Thunder,' but Simon, the one Jesus renamed Peter, truth be told, could outblast both of them together. The ground shook when he bellowed."

"Shook like the walls of Jericho?" Thomas asks in jest. He thinks he can safely indulge in lightheartedness with the two men now. More and more they're treating him as a fellow disciple rather than the devil's advocate.

"Our walls are still intact. So I'd say not," is Philip's equally congenial reply.

Thomas pats Philip's shoulder and smiles.

"There is a time for everything, as Solomon used to say," Philip offers.

"A time to listen and a time to learn," Thomas finishes the thought.

He finds himself enjoying the status quo. For, after all, do not all nine men share a common ground in being totally taken in by Jesus, totally befuddled by him? Each day's dawn brings fresh expectations, each day's dusk a fresh set of mysteries. Long they talk after turning in at night and ruminate on things he's said before finally drifting off to sleep. Even yet, however, Thomas yearns for a fully kindred soul, someone with whom he does not need to watch his manners, someone he can talk with about any thought that crosses his mind.

What churns their common curiosities now is what's ahead at Nazareth. Nathanael, who grew up in Cana, not two leagues away from there, can think of nothing other than a relaxed visit with Jesus' family. "Nothing good ever came out of there," he, however, still insists to those around him. "Hard to believe he did. Has to be something about it we don't know yet. Has to be. It's back country frozen in time. People are still living in caves there. Literally. Only difference between Nazarenes and their dogs is that the dogs are predictable."

Thomas does not argue—he's happy with the détente. Besides, he's never ventured into Nazareth and is reluctant to voice opinions on things he clearly knows nothing about and equally reluctant to elicit them from men who wear their biases like phylacteries.

But Philip does take issue. "We met his mother at the wedding feast," he tells his friend. "She came over from Nazareth. Quite civilized I'd say."

"The exception that proves the rule," says his best friend.

"And by all accounts so did he."

"You might have second thought by tomorrow," is all Nathanael says by way of retort.

On they trot.

Up until now Thomas has heard only good things about the town situated on a cliff overlooking a valley below where sheep can be seen dotting a landscape of green pastureland. When at length it comes into their view, it strikes him as more beautiful than described—the cliffside is more precipitous than he had imagined and the pasture with its snow-white ovines against a field of emerald green more picturesque.

Throughout their trek Jesus has seemed almost jubilant, looking to the right and left at his newest companions, chatting animatedly with them, even joking with them, himself chuckling wholeheartedly in the process. He has apparently been having a good time with all the men. Now abruptly, their destination in sight, he becomes totally silent; sad it seems to Thomas. Suddenly he is a man twice his age as he laboriously trudges on. The lilt is momentarily gone from his step, the good cheer from his lips.

"What does he see?" wonders Phillip out loud.

"Maybe what I see," offers Nathanael, "every time I try to visualize Nazareth."

"But it's lovely," says Thomas.

Nathanael shakes his head and almost whimsically says, "The village yes, but not the people. The surroundings, I have to admit, are quite attractive."

"What about people?"

"They have a well and a synagogue," Nathanael tells him. "The women congregate at the one, the men at the other—their conversations, no doubt, equally banal and equally provincial. Everyone knows everyone else. They tell folks it's a good place to raise a family, which is a barefaced lie. Until now, as I've already told you, nothing and no one good ever came out of Nazareth. Not a solitary single thing, I tell you. It's a collection of the most blah, primitive, little-minded, despicable people anywhere, capable of anything, less bright than their sheep, less gentle than their curs."

"He seemed so excited about getting us all down there. You could see it in his eyes."

"By tomorrow his eyes may tell another story."

Once inside the village, Jesus proceeds with his entourage to the house where he grew up and which his mother still calls home. There are people here and there along the way. They point excitedly to Jesus as he and his company make their way through the narrow streets. For some reason they seem to be expecting him. By sundown, the Sabbath's official commencement, the entire company is properly housed and fed.

The synagogue that next morning cannot be more crowded. Jesus arrives early, but even then the only seating the men can find are spaces here and there on benches at the rear of the building. At their master's beckoning, the disciples take those seats, while he himself goes up front where a bench is reserved for the rabbi of the day. There he sits and prays. Before long more people come. They squeeze in to jam every available space, elbow to elbow along the back and in the aisles.

Presently Jesus steps to the dais and looks out upon his audience. His eyes and demeanor tell Thomas that the sea of faces he gazes upon are both familiar and, for the time being, friendly. The synagogue attendant soon hands him the Scriptures. He unrolls the parchment and commences, loudly and emphatically, to read from the Book of the Prophet Isaiah a passage that speaks of the Christ:

The spirit of the Lord is upon me, because he hath anointed me to preach the gospel to the poor; he hath sent me to heal the brokenhearted, to preach deliverance to the captives and recovering of sight to the blind, to set at liberty them that are bruised, to preach the acceptable year of the Lord.

When he finishes reading, he returns the scroll to the attendant and sits down again. All eyes are fixed upon him, all bodies leaning his direction, heads cocked. Such stillness prevails that Thomas can hear his own heart beat. Not a soul in the room is stirring.

Jesus himself, rising in place, breaks the silence. "Today," he announces, "is this Scripture fulfilled in your hearing."

This brings a broad smile to Thomas's lips. He looks to his side where Andrew is seated. He also is smiling. Both glance sideways down the way at Nathanael. He is vigorously nodding his head, smiling more broadly than anyone in the synagogue. Thomas makes eye contact with him and the two nod approvingly to each other.

And then they focus again on Jesus, just as someone from the front of the synagogue calls out something to Jesus. Thomas cannot tell what the man is saying. Then it seems everyone wants to talk at once. Some wonder out loud what Jesus meant by his remark; others, especially those in back, welcome him warmly back home. An air of goodwill and camaraderie soon pervades the whole synagogue. Jesus is friendly and shows the same genuine interest in these people as he has everyone else so far. Thomas dares a sigh of relief. The occasion seems indeed a most auspicious one.

After the first wave of conversation, however, awkward silences begin to intrude; the people fidget in place, clearly not as much at ease as they were earlier. Jesus is still the focus of attention, but the men seem less interested now in what he is saying. He, for his part, continues to be as solicitous and cordial as earlier, but it slowly becomes apparent that this is not what the men wanted. It isn't why they've come.

No, not at all.

It's as though they're expecting something that just isn't happening, thinks Thomas. And gradually, because it isn't happening, some men are beginning to get upset. Even when they seem to try to be pleasant, their remarks are churlish and brusque. The cordiality that prevailed earlier is quickly evaporating. Several men stand up and start to pace.

One calls out to a friend across the room. "Why, it's only Joseph's son after all, isn't it?" he shouts.

The friend raises his eyebrows in agreement.

From elsewhere in the room others voice their assent, some none too softly. Thomas looks about the room. Jesus' disciples to a man seem taken aback. For some strange reason the local men are perturbed with Jesus, indeed visibly angry with him. So far he's done nothing to draw their fury; he still seems genuinely delighted to be back once more among his old friends and neighbors, but his friendliness is not being reciprocated.

Why? Thomas wants to know. Then quickly comes the moment when all conversation ceases at once, the ensuing silence saying best what hearts feel but tongues cannot articulate. All Thomas can hear are intermittent grumbles. Jesus, still on his feet, turns slowly in place, staring first at one group of men, then another and another.

"Oh, I hear what you're saying," he says to them, looking at his jeerers in their eyes. "You're saying, 'We've heard about all the things you did over at Cana and up at Capernaum. Now let's see you do the same things here. Give us a miracle, right here now in your own home city.' Why, that's it, isn't it? What you want is a miracle-worker, a magician maybe. You never heard a word I read or said, did you? You missed the greatest wonder of them all! You came here for a show, something to titillate your fancies and send thrills up and down your spines. Am I not right? You know I am."

The grumbling grows both in intensity and volume. Some men halfway own what he says; others show him their backs as if to deny it.

"Why, it's only the artisan's son!" Thomas hears them shouting louder, looking to their sides and back over their shoulders. "The artisan's son! The artisan's son acting high and mighty! We've known his family from way back. What's so special about him?"

Jesus, his face flush, responds in kind, loud enough to startle the sheep in the valley below. "A prophet is not without honor," he bellows back to them, "except in his own country! Thus it was in the days of Elijah; thus it was in the days of Elisha. Witness the Scriptures! And thus it is today! The miracles you seek shall not be forthcoming because you lack the faith to make them possible. You people lack the faith to make anything possible!"

Their anger now piqued by Jesus' outburst, the men suddenly close in upon him to seize him. That this is a synagogue and it is the Sabbath does not matter; these men, Jesus' onetime friends and neighbors, are momentarily not human beings at all but rather a pack of snarling, rabid jackals that would have their prey no matter what. Bent fingers, quivering with anger, reach out to clutch his wrists and arms and wrestle him toward a door.

Everyone in the building is now standing. Jesus' companions at the rear struggle to get to their master, but even those who would make way for them to get through cannot do so because the crowd is so tightly packed. Helplessly they look on as the men yank at Jesus' arms and drive their shoulders into him to force him through the doorway out onto the street.

Peter, with Thomas directly behind him, begins with all his strength to squeeze his way through the men blocking their way. Reaching out with his huge calloused hands, he grabs them at their shoulders and sweeps them to one side or the other, creating gaps just wide enough for him to lean in with his shoulder to wedge himself into their midst. Then planting his feet and pushing mightily, as if trying to loose a mud-mired fishing boat out into the lake, twisting his thick upper body, elbows flying, he heaves and heaves until there is give. Again and again he thrusts himself into and through the barricade of human bodies, Thomas still squeezing through the momentary wakes he's creating, until both are out of the door.

The street, also packed with people, is no easier to navigate than the synagogue. Repeatedly Peter, lowering his shoulder, with brute force plunges through the human herd to rescue the man they have known for only a few weeks but already own to be their master.

As the big man bends to position himself for another thrust, Thomas, still in tow, stands upright to look out over the heads of the rabble and spies the madmen half-dragging and half-pushing Jesus toward the drop-off at the edge of the village. Two brutish beings on either side grasp Jesus tightly at his wrists and forearms, their fingers, like raptor claws, dug into his skin. Two more, backs to their destination, are pulling strenuously at his robe, and one large man is in a crouch position behind Jesus pushing with all his power.

"They're heading for the cliff!" Thomas shouts.

Others are reaching in to prod him along the way. Between the two disciples and the rampageous would-be killers of Jesus is a horde of onlookers. Closer and closer the villains maneuver their prey toward the brow of the precipice.

Peter finds a new burst of energy and narrows the gap between them. He surges on through people who are no more than spectators, not part of the synagogue crowd at all— but ordinary people, ravenous for excitement, converging upon the scene to indulge their beastly appetites, folk who at other times would be finding their stimulation in dogfights or house fires.

Thomas can see ridges of rage in the mob leaders' foreheads and fire in their eyes as en masse they struggle to bring Jesus to the cliff's edge and begin to hoist him up to throw him over. Though happening in but an instant, the scene is almost in slow motion.

"No! No!" screams Peter as he makes one final full-body lunge, only to go sprawling less than a single cubit from the feet of Jesus' assailants.

But in a flash, in the blink of an eye, a most unreal thing happens. As Thomas looks on helplessly and Peter draws himself up from the ground, Jesus is suddenly quite literally shaking off his assailants. He flexes the muscles of his arms, raising them suddenly upward, and with smooth, apparently effortless motion twists his body around rapidly with the result that his back is now to the precipice and his face to the crowd. Grips are broken. He brushes hostile hands from his arms and wrists with the ease of an ordinary man brushing away loathsome insects or leeches.

Thomas gazes intently upon his face. It is rigid, his every muscle taut.

The men move in on Jesus and try to seize him a second time; but, as a great bull might charge through a flock of barnyard fowl, he shrugs them off like so many noxious vermin. He is not about to indulge his fellow townsmen's villainy any further. Standing tall, taller Thomas thinks than he's ever seen him, on through the ranks of the snarling curs and onlookers the Master walks toward his companions. Not a man reaches out with so much as a finger to touch him. Thomas and Peter quickly fall in behind him.

"He didn't need me," the fisherman tells his fellow disciple.

Thomas, elated as he has never been before, says, "Was that not something! From his own lips we heard it. From his own lips! 'Today is this Scripture fulfilled in your hearing.' Stupendous! Came right out and said it, Peter. The Christ is among us!"

At dawn that next morning Jesus and his disciples set out to return to Capernaum. With them are Jesus' mother and the members of her household, abandoning the town that for decades they have called home, probably never to return again. Theirs too has been a bittersweet adventure. They have seen men in frenzy, men they personally knew— some of whose houses were built by Mary's husband Joseph long ago, assisted by Jesus himself—reduced to the status of raucous, rabid animals. Man at his worst. They have also seen man at his best, one of their own, proffering hope and good will, crushed by rejection, triumphant when attacked. Man and manliness at their best.

This drama has not been lost on the men from Capernaum.

"An ox, an absolute ox," says Nathanael to Thomas, "most powerful man I've ever seen. At the end they opened up for him like the Red Sea. What a man!"

"They didn't hear a word he said," Philip adds. "All they wanted was a stunt like the one at Cana. Wanted a magic show. And when he didn't convert water into wine or wine into water or paving stones into gold, they became mad enough to kill him."

"Which they were not about to do. He's the Christ come at last!" Thomas again joins in. "Said it in so many words. Came right out and said it. The man's going to live forever."

"A lot to take in, though we've kind of known it all along," says John.

Peter soon draws up beside them. "Thought that's what he chose me for," he mumbles. "But he never needed me, did he? Never needed anybody."

"Halleluiah, what a day!" now says Thomas—to no one in particular. To himself most likely. "Makes you want to break out in song, doesn't it?"

"Don't think he needs a soul."

Philip leans into Thomas and in barely a whisper asks him, "Well, what's your verdict now, Twin?" he asks. "Miracle or providence?"

"It really doesn't matter, does it?" he tells him.

The train moves somberly, slowly toward Gennesaret. Elsewhere in its ranks other conversations are taking place. When the men speak, though, they soon do so in hushed tones, not because secrets are being shared but rather, more than likely, because the men do not want to intrude upon the musings of others. Thomas understands and for that reason labors to contain his own euphoria. The man was six hundred years in the coming, and now here he is. A day to leap into the air and click your heels!

Publicans and Sinners

THEY HAVE BEEN back in Capernaum several days now, venturing out into the hamlets and towns thereabouts. Jesus is still enlisting additional disciples. There are eleven men now in his train. For what purpose Thomas has no idea. However, fully aware of the Master's identity and convinced he does nothing without sound rationale, the man they still call the Twin is delighted to have the new fellows in their ranks.

Nathanael, who talks continually with Thomas now, always seems to know better than anyone else in the ranks of Jesus' disciples about what is going and who is who in Capernaum and the surrounding villages.

"He's a Zealot, you know," the metropolitan says almost in a whisper one evening, with a head gesture toward the young man immediately ahead of them, the Master's most recent recruit.

Thomas tells him he's heard that.

"Think he has it in his head Jesus will eventually be taking on the Romans. Grizzly crowd, those Zealots, them and the Sicarii. Fight fire with fire they insist on— except, when they say it, they're talking real flames. Met him yet?"

"Not to talk with," Thomas answers.

"Name's Simon. From what I can tell, he more or less seems to see his move from their camp to ours as pretty much a lateral one. Thinks our big thing's to send the Romans packing too. Jesus' apparently having his new kingdom all planned out after we've shaken off the Romans is apparently what tips his loyalties towards us."

"If Jesus picked him, he must have plans for him like all the rest of us," Thomas says, "although right now I'd have to say his strategy is still fuzzy at best."

"This is anything but a lateral move for him. That Zealot bunch is knee-deep in covert warfare—sabotage, carnage, whatever it takes. And, unless I'm gravely mistaken, I don't think we are. They're back to 'Saul killed his thousands and David his tens of thousands.' And, to hear some of them talk, they're hoping to kill their hundreds of thousands as well. Anything and everything's fair play."

"They certainly misestimate the Roman Empire."

"And, more important to us, they misunderstand everything Jesus so far has said."

"Our young colleague will soon figure out, I'm sure, that Jesus' kingdom may well turn into much more than simply a restoration of a kingdom that existed a thousand years ago," Thomas tells his fellow.

"I know that and you know that, but right now I don't think young Simon knows it. And who's to say what he might do in the name of us all before he figures it out? Could have a problem on our hands."

"He'll probably catch on right quickly."

"I only hope sooner rather than later."

Thomas, uncomfortable about the direction their conversation seems to be going, asks Nathanael about another of Jesus' new picks. "Any apprehensiveness about the Judean?" he says.

"Nothing so far. Seems quite in earnest to me."

On their way back to Capernaum from nearby Chorazin that following day Thomas does pick up his pace so that he is near the front of the pack so he can stroll beside Simon the Zealot. Only the big man Peter, still the bodyguard, is between them and Jesus himself.

"I'm Thomas in case you didn't know," he announces as he draws even with the newcomer. "You'll hear some of our fellows call me the Twin, but it's Thomas. They'll tell you I might be a Greek, but that's wrong too. As Israelite as old Jacob himself."

"Me too," the younger man tells him.

"And the man leading us, in case you haven't heard, is the Christ of God. Never let anybody mislead you about him either. Everybody here except you and the Judean back there heard him virtually declare it in a synagogue down in Nazareth in so many words. Read a passage from the Book of Isaiah about the Christ and said, 'This day this Scripture is fulfilled.' In other words, 'I'm the man!' So he said he is, and he acts and sounds the part. Wondered if you knew that."

"It's why I'm here," Simon tells him, "that and, of course, the fact he invited me."

"Invited or commanded? I've never been sure."

"Good distinction. I don't know either."

"Talks about God like he knows Him personally," Thomas, smiling, goes on. "Seems to have tons to tell us and, as our friends here will let you know, seems to have the power of God in his fingertips. But beware, he's full of surprises."

"You were down there in Nazareth and heard him firsthand when he declared himself to be the Christ?"

"That I was."

"Then you must have seen what happened when they tried to murder him right after. A gang of heavyweights manhandled him right up to the edge of the cliff, and he brushed their hands from his arms and legs like they were noxious gnats and tromped straight back through the middle of them as if they were no more than a flock of lambs. That must have been something! And you were right there."

"You could say I was third in line."

"Really? Yes, must have been something."

"What he said inside the synagogue was a bigger something: 'I'm the Christ!' That was the flash of lightning for me. What happened at cliffside was fading thunder, maybe confirming the lightning but aeons from adding to it. Lightning gives you a fleeting glimpse of what's out there; thunder's the sound effect when it hits you later."

"The man's identity's what matters, not his powers. That your point?"

Thomas nods. "Given who he is, you can expect almost anything. As I say, there'll be a ton of surprises down the road for us. That you can count on. I truly think we might well be in the presence of the greatest thing our nation's never known."

"So it's Kingdom of God, here we come!"

"You might put it that way, but there's no guarantee the path will be an easy one. There will be enemies ahead every bit as dogged as those who tried to kill him down there. That I fully expect. And a whole lot more devious and cunning. He'll need the strength of a thousand bulls to charge through them. Who knows? Maybe ten thousand."

"And who, in your judgment, will these enemies be?"

"Other people he refuses to do magic stunts for probably, others who for some reason will look upon him as threat of some kind?"

"The Romans and their minions?"

"Among others closer to us. Those down in Nazareth certainly weren't Romans. I'm not even sure the Romans know Nazareth exists."

"You think the whole country, north and south, will fall in and rally to his side? Could be a bloody mess before it's all over. They won't go down easy. I don't know much, but I do know that much."

Their conversation continues in this vein as Jesus and his eleven disciples are nearing one of the main portals leading into Capernaum. As they are about to enter the city's east gate, Thomas finds himself momentarily distracted by the sight just ahead of a tax booth and the repugnant face of Levi Matthew, its proprietor, at the window. Matthew's is the face everyone sees upon coming into the city from the west. He is a publican among publicans, harvester of taxes in the service of Rome, albeit, insist some, one of the fairer ones in that sector. He lives well but not ostentatiously so. Such is Thomas's assessment at any rate. Anyone else in his position would be as rich as Croesus.

But he is a publican, and every man in the city at one time or another has been forced to plunk down his purse of hard-earned denarii on the table of his booth. Being less villainous than others of his ilk does little to allay the rancor of those forced to leave his establishment lighter of loose change than when they approached it.

Those not in arrears with their taxes, however, are not accosted. They can pass right on by the man without so much as a nod of their heads in acknowledgment of his miserable existence. Such is the case now with the Nazarene and his company. But Jesus stops anyway right in front of the tax collector's table and his disciples with him. Matthew glances up at him.

For an instant Jesus fixes the publican with his eyes, then says to him as he has previously said to eleven other men, "Follow me!"

The men around Jesus stand stock-still, Thomas no less than the others, wondering if they've heard correctly. Matthew rises immediately and, leaving all his coins sitting on the table, rushes out of the booth quickly to Jesus' side. With the publican now with them, the men continue on their way toward the marketplace.

Even Thomas has to raise a careful eyebrow over this. "That makes twelve of us," he says to Nathanael, now coming up beside him, "same as the number of tribes Moses long ago led out of Egypt into the Promised Land. Don't you wonder, is truth were told, if he worked it out so every tribe's represented?"

"Didn't occur to me till you mentioned it," says his friend. "Different kind of journey though, different kind of Promised Land."

"Yes, a vaguer and more remote Promised Land, but, I dare say, we might have just stepped into a vaguer and more remote wilderness too by taking one of its native scavengers into our tent. But the man, they tell me, is as good a man as any that ever sat behind a tax table."

"That I grant," Simon the Zealot comes in, "but isn't that like saying a given vulture is good because it pecks at our flesh more kindly than others. He's still a vulture."

"I'm sure Jesus has his reasons."

"He no doubt has his reasons, I grant you, but his reasons in this case seem a little opaque. At best this publican's a bloodsucker, a leech, a sellout to Rome. Why him? Of what earthly use can a lackey of Caesar be in building the Kingdom of God?"

To this Thomas shrugs his shoulders and makes a sweep of his hand toward his fellow disciples. "Of what earthly use can any of us be?"

"Of some use I would certainly hope."

"Take inventory, will you. Look at us! Fishermen, gadabouts, workmen, petty merchants, establishmentarians, and disestablishmentarians—ordinary men from ordinary walks of life. The closest we have to a natural leader is someone who used to bark orders to his fellow fishermen out on the lake, whose primary and maybe sole talent is a loud voice. None of us makes any sense."

"A lot more sense than he," says the Zealot, shrugging his head toward Levi Matthew.

Thomas does not respond to the gesture.

Later that same day toward evening Jesus and all his disciples and not a few of Matthew's fellow tax collectors and friends, all very much of his own stamp, gather for dinner at the erstwhile publican's house. It becomes quickly obvious that none of Jesus' close companions has ever rubbed shoulders with such a collection of sinners in their whole lives. Their fathers, opines Thomas, would be shocked out of their skins.

However, Jesus himself seems perfectly at ease eating and drinking and laughing with this company. This much does make a modicum of sense. After all, did not the citizens of Jesus' own hometown only a few days earlier turn their backs on him to the point that they tried to murder him? These people now about them are at least a cut above them. In ways more lepers than the lepers themselves, these lowly souls seem genuinely thrilled to be in Jesus' presence and do not need tricks or magic stunts to make them listen to what he has to say.

The Judean, whose name Thomas has learned is Iscariot, is seated beside the Zealot, who in turn sits directly across from Thomas himself. No one in the courtyard, in dress or demeanor, seems so out of place as he. Judas is his given name. Thomas eyes him as he glances furtively up and down the table, first directly at him and then at those on either side.

He is clearly uncomfortable.

All of the other guests are from the coastal towns and villages around Gennesaret, most from right there in Capernaum, and clearly half of them from the ranks of men the Judean normally crossed the street to avoid. There is an air about Judas that suggests he has just inadvertently stumbled into a party of highwaymen and is desperate for some route by which to make quick exit. Finding none, he leans in toward Simon the Zealot to strike up a conversation.

Soon the eastern sky darkens and torches are brought on. Thomas looks at others about him and is struck by the dumbfounded looks on all of their faces. Up and down the table there is palpable bewilderment. Judas may not be so much the odd man out after all.

There seated at the table of honor is Jesus, surrounded by his host and his host's business and social cronies, eating and drinking and laughing and apparently having a good time of it. Nothing at the table so much as hints of impropriety or compromise—new friends, now good friends, enjoying each other's company, that's all.

"Down our way this'd be branded sin of major consequence at very least," Iscariot blurts out, "if not out and out treason."

Simon the Zealot seems torn. "Same up here in some circles, but I'm told the man's full of surprises. There's reason behind everything he does."

"I'm sure there is, but what conceivable strategy do you think can be served by this most unholy of alliances?"

"No apparent strategy at all," says Simon. "But that's more likely a comment on the limitations of our own imaginations than it is his overall scheme. Believe me, I'm no more comfortable than you are and have every intention of keeping my distance for the time being. Two weeks ago I might have consented to half the lot's being stoned to death. But who's to know? He seems to be enjoying their company. The man's God's emissary. Maybe he's saying something to the rest of us. Who knows what that is?"

Thomas, not entirely comfortable himself, says a muted "Amen."

"Our emerging king skips over the cream and goes for the lees at the bottom of the bucket," the Judean says next, glancing to his right at Simon the Zealot, who now seems to be looking elsewhere. "Weird strategy. That's all I can say. Hope that doesn't define the kingdom we'll all some day be helping to govern."

Young Simon continues to look off into the distance. As the last traces of daylight disappear, he seems to see something behind the hedgerow at the open end of Levi Matthew's courtyard. His focus fixes on the hedgerow.

The conversation among those at their table momentarily ceases. Elsewhere around them there are audible murmurs, but Thomas cannot gauge their tenor. The chatter at the head table, however, is lively and at moments outrightly boisterous. Those nearest Jesus and their host all seem to be talking at once, their prattle punctuated at points by spontaneous peals of laughter.

Judas conspicuously nudges the Zealot with his elbow. "Know what I call that?" he asks him.

"What."

"Humor among thieves. What's your take?"

"I don't know," the young man answers, still studying the growing darkness beyond them. "At the moment frankly I'm not sure I know anything. Seems a little unreal I guess. I was always told these kinds of people have all made pacts with the devil, that they've bartered away their souls for filthy lucre, that they're betrayers of kind, bleeders of brethren for the moneybags of Rome, forsaken by God himself."

"What I've been told too."

"And that they are the very ones we need the Christ to save us from. I honestly don't know what this means."

Simon's voice, though barely above a whisper, is heavy with emotion. It is not bitterness Thomas discerns in it or even disappointment as much as perplexity. And that he can understand.

At the head table there is another round of laughter, more raucous than the one preceding it. Simon the Zealot remains glum and speechless; he is at the moment a man at war within himself, struggling to mask his true feelings, fully aware that he is failing in the effort.

Judas Iscariot at his side is clearly in silent dialogue with himself, pensive at one instant, almost smirking the next. Thomas can see his lips moving. Now he nods. "Yes, yes, I see it," the Judean blurts out loud.

"See what?" the Zealot wants to know.

"The man's strategy, why he's playing Absalom to this nest of scoundrels"

"And what could that strategy be?"

"Simply that he knows he'll be needing them and, in all probability, right soon."

"Need them?" responds young Simon. "Need them for what?"

"Shekels, my lad! Shekels!" Iscariot tells him as well as others within earshot. "You don't build the grandest kingdom ever seen with scraps and pieces. Nosirree! You need coin, my fellow, buckets and buckets of coin, coin by the wagons full. And these guys here are the ones who've got it and know where there's whole lot more."

"Lookee here!" says the Zealot, perplexity suddenly giving way to surprise in his eyes. "I knew somebody was there."

Thomas wheels himself around to see five men drift into the courtyard and begin to mill about the area. He instantly recognizes them. By their robes and the broad phylacteries strapped to their foreheads and left arms, even the nonlocals have to know exactly who they are and probably why they are crashing this festivity.

They advance, almost in step, to the foot of the disciples' table, close enough so that Thomas, if he wants to, can reach out and touch the man leading the way. They are by no means sheepish in their intrusion. All stand erect, their shoulders squared. Their countenances all bear the same crooked noses, furrowed brows, rigid jawlines and taut chins—every one of them, one could imagine, having been chiseled from the same stone by the same sculptor.

The three foremost among them, Thomas sees, are definitely Pharisees. The other two, both slightly younger, are apparently theologians. As others at the gala gradually become aware of the uninvited guests, a hush falls over the festivities.

"You!" barks their spokesman, glaring at Peter. Then, nodding in the direction of the head table, "You follow this man?" It's more a statement than a question.

"That I do," responds Peter unequivocally.

"Then, tell me, why is it that you people choose these tax collectors and their fellow vermin, the dregs of our little world, to be your dinner companions?" the Pharisee presses loudly for all to hear. "Bloodsuckers, you have to know, betrayers of their own kind, is what they are! Everybody knows it. And with them you elect to rub shoulders and break bread. Have you no shame?"

Peter does not respond to this tirade.

But Jesus does. Without standing and with modulated voice, he says, "Your question, sir, I realize as does everybody else in your hearing, is for me. Allow me, if you will, to answer it."

"What are you doing here?" asks the Pharisee, as if taken aback.

"Who is it that needs a doctor?" Jesus ask him. "Is it the healthy person or the sick one? I think we can agree, can we not, that it is definitely the one who is ill."

"Yes," says the man, "but. . . ."

"By the same token," Jesus breaks him off, "I did not come to change the ways of spiritually vigorous, righteous, upstanding men such as yourself, sir, nor your zealous companions here either. I came for these people, those you see seated about me. You say they are sinners, and you're right. They are. No one is more conscious of that than they are themselves, which is precisely, you have to understand, why I can address their needs and not yours."

"One thing I do understand," the Pharisee retorts, "is that you wouldn't catch the Baptizer carousing around in this company. That much I do know. He and his disciples are forever fasting and praying, not tippling with scum and damnable lowlifes, gorging themselves with all kinds of delicacies."

"You want John the Baptizer dead, and yet you hold him up as an example!"

"But you yourself think him to be a prophet, do you not?" argues the Pharisee. "Why then do you not emulate him?"

"To be sure, he is a prophet," Jesus says, "the greatest prophet of them all. His mission is not mine though. What you see here is a coming together, a celebration. If you will, try to think of it as a wedding, which, beyond your knowing, it indeed is."

"I see neither bride nor bridegroom," replies the model of rectitude, glancing conspicuously around the courtyard. "You know, the one thing, maybe the only thing, I've always admired about the Baptizer is that he's never cryptic or abstruse. One does not have to be a riddle-master to understand what he has to say."

Ignoring the sarcasm, Jesus finishes making his point. "A wedding's not an occasion for fasting," he says. "As long as the bridegroom is still on the scene, it is a time, as I say, for celebration and merriment—for tippling, as you put it— and the devouring of tasty food. Oh, there'll be time for prayer and fasting all right, after he's gone, but not now. Not now, gentlemen."

The Pharisees and theologians linger but briefly after this exchange and then leave.

There is a lull after the intruders' exodus before the gala's tempo regains its original pitch. Twitters graduate quickly into chatter and chatter into general hubbub. Although a few conversations merely seem to pick up from where they've been interrupted by the party crashers, the focus of attention at most tables quickly shifts to the uninvited visitors themselves. Thomas can hear expressions of outrage in some quarters and disgust in others; attempts at ridicule and notes of apprehensiveness and alarm in still others.

In due time it is Jesus' allusion to a wedding that becomes the chief topic of conversation and conjecture. "He did call this a wedding, didn't he?" Judas Iscariot asks.

"We all heard him," says the Zealot.

"You think then our King of kings and Lord of lords is looking at a time when he'll have a queen at his side?"

"Sees himself as the bridegroom. That much was clear."

"It's just metaphor," interrupts Thomas. "He loves metaphor. Our thing here tonight is *like* a wedding feast, not literally one. That's all."

At that moment laughter once more breaks from the head table, spontaneous and hearty, followed by relative quiet as Jesus rises to his feet to entertain those immediately around him with stories. Those in proximity cock their heads and lean forward so as not to miss a single word he speaks. Some seem to be getting whatever points he's trying to make, others merely enjoying the stories for their own sakes. Thomas takes note that their host, Levi Matthew, seems to be among the former.

The chatter of those around him has shifted from metaphors to Pharisees. The men seem to be of one mind in their satisfaction of Jesus' handling of the local elitists who barged into their soiree. Nathanael and Philip, imitating the Pharisees' sanctified tones, recall verbatim the questions they asked and then Jesus' mellow, matter-of-fact answers.

The Judean and the Zealot speculate about the intruders' motivations and others about their designs for future encounters. In low tones they seem to be agreeing that battle lines have now been drawn and that this has been the first of many skirmishes. A war of sorts has been waged, and neither is sure how it will be played out. Things are about to happen.

The Pharisees and theologians, however, have not completely abandoned the current scene. When the festivities are later breaking up and the guests are leaving, all five are still there just beyond the gates, accosting the disciples as they pass by, incessantly asking each one, "Why's he eating with tax collectors and all those other reprobates?"

"I told you!" Jesus, immediately behind his disciples, snaps. "It is not the healthy and hale who need a doctor, but the sick. I did not come to call the righteous but sinners to repentance!"

"Our future has just arrived," Thomas can hear Judas tell the Zealot.

"So it seems."

"But, mind you, these local Pharisees and theologians are no more than scruffy country roosters compared to the strutting peacocks he'll have to square off against down in Judea, which I think is where we'll soon be headed," Judas, the man of experience, continues glumly. "Their brethren down there, believe you me, are brighter and a whole lot more vicious and devious. And they will never walk away, never ever give him a moment's slack whatsoever. If he doesn't crush them, they'll crush him."

"Then he will surely crush them," Simon the Zealot says, confidence in his voice. "That I believe with all my heart."

"Remember he's got to take on the whole Roman Empire as well."

"He'll do that too. One of these days, maybe not the first time we go down there, but one of these days, we will see him astride a white charger galloping triumphantly through the gates of Jerusalem to take his throne."

"That your prophecy?"

"That it is! Crowds a hundred deep will surge into the thoroughfares and streets, throwing orchids and palms and silken mantles before him, and cry out their hosannas so boisterously they'll echo off the bluffs up and down the River Jordan and stir ripples on the still bays of Gennesaret. That'll happen. I can just see it. And when it does, the theologians and Pharisees and all the legions of Rome will bow down before him."

Up the Mountain

A S THEY COMMENCE climbing the mountain, the men are still talking about John the Baptizer's imprisonment by King Herod. Several have heard the prophet in person, and three have actually counted themselves in the ranks of his disciples. That the legendary, quaintly attired, gaunt outdoorsman should be confined to a dungeon cell at all seems to them a punishment far out of proportion to his crime of simply calling sin by its proper name.

"Apparently one doesn't tag the Tetrarch an adulterer and get off with a warning," says Thomas.

"Especially if he insists on shouting it from the rooftop," Levi Matthew, the onetime tax collector now at Thomas's side, adds.

"Called the Pharisees a brood of vipers down in Judea," John tells them. "He's blunt with people. That's all. That's what he does, calls out sin. The Pharisees, not as thin-skinned as our own Herod, quietly slunk back to the Temple."

"Herod might have settled for being called a viper too," Philip comes in, "but not a violator of his brother's bed. Too specific. That was pointing the same finger at his mistress. Very likely the Baptizer's arrest was not so much the King's initiative as hers."

John agrees. "A true viper that one, fangs and all."

"She also has a seductive daughter, a dancer they say, who's part of the package she brought here with her. Salome. Can cast a spell over Herod at will. They're a pair, that one and her mother. I do fear for our friend. I truly do."

The opinions of others are less pessimistic. Most theorize that Herod merely wants to terrorize the Baptizer and his entourage so that at very least he'll retreat back south to the Jordan and never again venture into Galilee.

"That'll never happen," says John. "The man's not about to be intimidated by anybody."

From what Thomas has seen and heard, he has to agree with that. The Baptizer will offer his throat to whomever he offends, but he is not about to have his lips sealed. He'll ride it out irrespective of where it takes him. He's a man he would have liked to meet.

Gradually the conversation turns from the fate of John the Baptizer to what they're now doing—to wit, climbing this mountain. The pathway to its foot is broad enough for two or three to walk abreast, but now, as they ascend, it has quickly narrowed. At points here and there they have to go single file. Where the ground is soft and the dirt loose they can see dozens of hoofprints left by goats and sheep in their migrations to more lush pastures nearer the top. Jesus leads the way.

Among those momentarily at the end of the procession, it is Thomas who raises the big question. "Anybody know what this is about?" he asks.

"Could be the stairway to heaven for all I know," offers Nathanael, immediately ahead of him. "If it is, we've still got a bit of a climb left."

Judas Iscariot, behind Thomas, gets in his shekel's worth. "And the goats seem to have a leg up on us again."

"Figuratively speaking, it well could be," offers Matthew. "Whatever he's got to say is for us and us alone. Later maybe for the rest of the country, but right now only for us, being his own private flock."

Thomas ponders this. "Something seems afoot," he says, as he takes advantage of the path's widening to lag back with Levi Matthew. "Definitely a change in the winds."

Matthew does not respond to this directly. Instead he asks Thomas if he thinks there's a connection between the Baptizer's arrest and their now being led up the mountain. "Some of the men seem to think John may not be the only dissident they'll be tossing into the dungeon."

"So we're on the run to separate ourselves from the Baptizer—'s that it?"

"Little rumble, no more. I seriously doubt if our Tetrarch is even aware of our existence at this point," Matthew says. "Some word of Jesus' alleged miracles might possibly have reached him—which, one, he doesn't buy and, two, even if he does, there is absolutely no scent of sedition about Jesus whatsoever. No, I don't think our mountain climbing has anything to do with Herod."

"And not with the Baptizer's incarceration either?"

"That I don't know. The Baptizer, the great prophet of our own time—if you asked Jesus, the greatest ever—is suddenly put on hold, at least for the time being, just as the man we believe to be the Christ has finally picked his key standard-bearers and is about to clue them in on the nature of his kingdom and his strategies to bring it into existence. Is that coincidence? I don't know. Could the day of the prophets be over and a new day, that of a far greater than David, about to be born? That I do not know either, but I must say the thought of it intrigues me like nothing in my life ever has."

"Something's up. This is definitely a lot more than your average walk in the woods."

"Your wishful thinking, I see, has made you giddy."

"Nobody's ever accused me of being giddy. Maybe a little excited, that's all," Thomas says; then, nodding toward the Zealot and the Judean just ahead of them, adds, "They're the ones that are giddy, not me."

"That they definitely are, but so are you. You simply hide it better than anybody that's ever lived."

"The ironic thing is they both think they're ideological soul mates, but the one dreams about being a viceroy and the other a regicide. Can't help but overhear them sometimes, they talk so exuberantly."

"I still say you're giddy."

"Only hopeful. Huge things are about to happen. I do feel it in my bones."

"You feel it in your bones, you say? I did not take you for a man of intuition, Thomas."

"I'm not. 'Intuition' suggests conclusion without intelligible foundation; 'gut-feeling' or 'hunch' the unsophisticated would call it. 'Whim' maybe. The feeling of which I speak derives from my observations of Jesus: the inherent wisdom in everything I've so far heard him say, his aura of authority, the utter mystery of the man himself. You'd think sometimes he actually knows the great Lord God personally. You know the Scriptures, Levi, better than anybody in his train. Does he not measure up almost perfectly to the picture of the Christ painted by the prophets?"

"More so than anybody I've ever heard of," Matthew responds, "though we know almost nothing about his birth or boyhood. There are prophecies about his birth, you know, that might give us pause to wonder. But, yes, he does speak as though the authority of God is behind every word he utters."

"He's the one we've waited six hundred years for. I truly believe that with every fiber of my being."

Of all his fellows Thomas finds himself most comfortable now with the erstwhile publican. He is astonished by Matthew's grasp of the Scriptures, far exceeding that of the theologians he has oftentimes encountered. For all intents and purposes he has to have scrolls of the Laws and Prophets fully memorized—not that he ever set out to do that, but it must have somehow happened because of his much study.

"A man of my profession isn't encumbered by a lot of social life," the publican confided in him early on. "You've got time for other things."

"No close friends?" he asked him on that occasion.

"Other publicans, but superficial friends at best. A Roman administrator that dropped by every other week or so to pick up Caesar's share—had a cup of wine with him when he wasn't in too much hurry. Lepers, Samaritans, Greeks, and others of my ilk."

Matthew invariably makes light of it when the topic comes up. He has a good sense of humor, which Thomas appreciates, knowing personally that sorrow rather than joy is the secret source of wit.

Funny people more often than not are from the ranks of the shy, the weird, the rejected, the socially awkward, the misunderstood, the abused and the frail. It doesn't necessarily work the other way, however; not all outcasts and rejects are funny. Some compensate in other ways. Some are simply pathetic.

Matthew, having a couple years or so on Thomas, is roughly the same height. He is not what you'd call a handsome person but could be labeled nice looking or maybe just not bad looking. His shoulders are a little rounded; his nose and Adam's apple would probably get mentioned if one were describing him for some reason. The twenty or so pounds he has on Thomas are not of muscle; he is not a man you would find on Gennesaret throwing out fishing nets or at a forge shaping iron with a hammer. He dresses neatly, wears no jewelry, emits no foul odors, is soft spoken and polite. And he can think. Thomas finds much in the man to like.

They trudge on up the mountain now side by side, their shoulders almost touching where the path narrows again. Thomas could not ask for better company. Soon they have to walk single file once more but only for a short distance. Then, when party pauses in a clearing to rest under the bow of a huge cedar, the two men again find themselves standing next to each other.

Levi Matthew turns to Thomas. His face glows with high expectation. "Moses went up a mountain once too, you remember," he says, "and, when he came down, he carried the Commandments that shaped a nation. Ask me what's running through my head right now, that would be it. "

"You think Jesus will do the same?"

"Perhaps. The man's an original. He's apparently got the disciples he wanted, although I must confess I can't figure out why he chose any of us. Not a man of distinction in the whole lot. Collection of blank slates, that's all. But that too, I have a feeling, is about to change. Things are happening, my friend. You're on target there. Things are definitely happening. Exactly what is anybody's guess."

Soon they're back on the path and, before long, come upon an emerald knoll. Grazing animals, now doubtlessly in pastures well above them, have recently chewed the bushes and grass down so that new growth carpets the natural shelf. There they stop. The ground slopes in places, and there are rocks and a fallen tree trunk where the men can sit down, which Jesus invites them to do. He himself, however, chooses to stand and wander amidst them.

Up until this point Jesus has proven most affable. One could not help but like him. The men have seen him jolly, as at Levi Matthew's party, able to engage their interests with stories and good humor with an unexpected mix of irony and comic exaggeration. He's been animated, often getting his hands and eyes and a thousand different facial contortions into his narratives. There have been times when they haven't been sure when to laugh and when not to.

This soon becomes one of those times. He begins his discourse, almost as a preamble, with a litany of what seem a series of paradoxes, one after the other. Almost rhapsodically, poetically, like David in some of his psalms, he tells them how wonderfully privileged all the riff-raff are because they already possess the kingdom of heaven and how wonderfully privileged likewise are the poverty-stricken because they're about to inherit the earth.

Holding back their laughter, the disciples study his eyes for some sign that he's putting them on, but there is none.

Thomas, sitting across from Iscariot, sees the Judean cock his eyebrows and scratch his head as Jesus continues. His jaw drops as if in disbelief. Then his cheeks tighten to suggest an oncoming smile as he leans forward to respond in laughter if indeed it should turn out that Jesus is pulling their legs, this followed by cocked eyebrows again when it's suddenly apparent to the man that their master is in dead earnest.

"And the bereaved—how wonderfully privileged they are because they will find comfort!" Jesus continues. "And those hungry for goodness because they're going to be filled to the gills! And those persecuted in the pursuit of what's right because their payoff's going to be the kingdom of God itself!"

Once more Thomas sees Judas Iscariot's mouth drop wide

open—then, nudging the Patriot next to him, softly says something. Thomas can't tell what. The Patriot doesn't react.

"And how wonderfully privileged are you, my friends, when people falsely accuse you and slander you incessantly and punish you for my sake!" Jesus finishes, looking each in the eyes. "Then is the time to explode with joy, for your reward in heaven will be truly magnificent!"

He then wanders off by himself into a grove of acacias adjacent to the knoll.

"Is he dreaming or am I?" says Thomas to Matthew. "I'm sorry, but the world he describes, where the downtrodden all come out winners, seems a bit askew from the real one. He's somewhere else completely."

"Aptly put," Matthew responds. "He's in his dreamworld all right, but take heed. That dreamworld's apparently the world by which he measures what we call 'the real world' and finds it wanting. It's also, I'd guess, the world he hopes to bring into being, to wit, his own upcoming kingdom. More than a tad idealistic, I'd say."

"Whatever that entails."

"We'll find out about that quickly enough. He's coming back."

Thomas glances toward the acacias to see Jesus emerging. The Master still chooses to stand and shift about rather than sit on the boulder immediately behind him. Earlier, when he delivered his curious list of wonderfully privileged people, he was the crier of good fortune, ebullient, beaming. He is now the rabbi, with prologue behind him, getting down to lesson time.

"You, my dear men, are the salt of the earth," in heavier tones he goes on to say, "which necessitates, of course, that your rectitude must exceed that of the Pharisees and theologians."

"What's that?" says the Zealot in a whisper loud enough for all to hear.

"He just said we need to be more perfect than perfect," says Judas Iscariot equally loudly.

"How can that be? The Pharisees abide by the Commandments

to the very letter. It's what they do. It's their profession. If something's even remotely questionable, they steer a wide arc around it."

"Well, you men must do better," says Jesus, apparently hearing this. "Abide by the spirit of the Law as well as by the letter. And do not imagine that, because of recent happenstances, I'm here to scuttle the Law or the Prophets. Oh no, not for one moment. Absolutely not! I am here to reemphasize them, not throw them to the winds. Know that! Heaven and earth, I tell you, will pass away before a single line or even one teeny letter of the Law is rendered null and void.

"You men must go to the very heart and soul of the Commandments. Let me explain. One of the Commandments says, *Thou shalt not murder.* What I'm telling you is that whoever harbors murderous rage against his fellow man risks the judgment of God. And so also does anyone who holds his brother in malicious contempt. So do not be offering up sacrifices to God while there is still enmity between you and your brother. First make peace with him. And then, and only then, approach the altar of God."

"That's not what we've always been told," says someone behind Thomas.

"I repeat. It is the spirit of the Law, more than the letter, that is crucial," Jesus goes on. "Along the same vein, you've heard the commandment, *Thou shalt not commit adultery*, have you not? Well, I'm telling you that any man who ogles a woman in lust has effectively already committed adultery with her in his heart. Better for him to rip out first one eye and then the other than to trash his whole eternal existence."

Hyperbole, thinks Thomas. *Linguistic overkill to drive home the point. Very effective. Lust is serious business, one of Solomon's Seven Deadly Sins. It's not to be taken lightly, not the stuff of wit and jest. Shouldn't be painted blazing red but ugly black.*

Jesus goes on to set down stricter standards for divorce than Moses did. Then he takes to task the idea of any kind of oath. "Don't swear by anything," he tells them. "Don't swear by heaven, for it is the throne of God; nor by earth, for that is his footstool. Do not even swear by your own head, for that is not in your control either. A simple 'yes' or 'no' will do fine. Anything more is wrong.

"You have heard it said, *An eye for an eye and a tooth for a tooth*, have you not? Well, what I say is do not counter evil with evil. If anybody whacks you on the right cheek, turn to him your left also. If anybody hauls you into court to take your coat, give him your cloak as well. If he strong-arms you into going a mile, go another one on your own. Give to any man who asks of you anything, and never turn down anyone who seeks to borrow.

"And I know you've been told, *Thou shalt love thy friend and hate thine enemy.* I say love your enemies also and bestow your blessings upon those who run roughshod over everything you hold dear. Do that and you will be true sons of your Heavenly Father. There is no distinction in loving only those who love you. The rogues out there do that much. Being nice only to those in your own circle is nothing special. That might be an achievement for pagans, but not you. You must do better. Let your Father in Heaven be your standard."

These are the beginnings of things he tells them on the mountain that day. There are more, all of them things Thomas and no doubt his fellows as well look upon as hard things, things that stick to their insides and cause their bowels to churn. Their Christ is turning out to be a hard and demanding taskmaster after all.

Up until this discourse he has chided them, told them story upon story, spoken vaguely of the Kingdom of God; he has healed invalids and spoken kindly to them and shown himself a friend to the downtrodden. Except that his disciples keep pace with him on the road and not lag behind, he has not defined a difficult course for them at all.

That ride, Thomas realizes, is definitely over. "Heavy stuff," he says to Levi Matthew, as Jesus retreats to the acacia grove again.

"He simply wants us to be more like him."

Jesus quickly returns. Still the rabbi, he goes on to say, "What you are is the light of the world. I intend that you be seen. People don't go around lighting lamps and then sticking buckets over them, do they? No, they place them conspicuously on lamp-stands so their families and neighbors can see. Even so, let your light so shine before men that they might catch sight of your good deeds and give glory to your Father in Heaven.

"But when you do your acts of kindness, do so inconspicuously. Don't trumpet your own good deeds like the grandstanders you see posturing in the synagogues and streets. They pander for public recognition, which, I tell you, is all the reward they'll ever get. Perform your labors of love with a certain sleight of hand—don't even let your left hand know what the right is doing. Your Father, who sees in secret, will reward you openly.

"And this goes for prayer as well. The phonies just love to loiter around the synagogues and street corners and pray and pray and pray—all so people can see them. When you pray, go into a room and shut the door and raise your prayers to your Father in privacy. And don't rattle off a whole string of empty phrases clothed in pious palaver as the Gentiles do, thinking they'll be answered because of the sheer quantity of their words. Rest assured. God, who is your Father, already knows what you need. Let this be your model:

> *Our Father who art in Heaven, hallowed by thy name;*
> *thy kingdom come, thy will be done on earth as it is in Heaven.*
> *Give us this day our daily bread.*
> *Forgive us our debts as we forgive our debtors.*
> *Lead us not into temptation, but deliver us from evil,*
> *for thine is the kingdom and the power and the glory forever.*

"And keep this in mind—that, if you forgive others, your Heavenly Father will forgive you. But if you don't, he won't.

"Oh yes, and when you fast, leave off those hangdog faces the grandstanders are always putting on. They dishevel their hair and suck in their cheeks. And, all bent over, heads drooped, jaws slackened, mouths wide-open, tongues dangling like those of street curs, they squint catatonically at their sandals, now and then glancing furtively about, of course, to make sure everybody takes notice and accords them proper respect."

As he says this, Jesus—suddenly the performer, the animated storyteller—sucks in his own cheeks and exaggeratedly contorts his face and physique to mimic the hypocrites he's describing. His disciples, hungry for something to laugh at, laugh perhaps more boisterously than the mimicry warrants.

"No, no, no!" he says, while still in pose. Then, straightening up, with the hint of a smile at the corners of his lips, "When you fast, my friends, wash your faces and brush your hair neatly. Stand erect and put a little spring in your step. No one should so much as guess that you're fasting. Your Father in Heaven is the only one who needs to know."

Jesus lets this sink in. Throughout his discourse he has been standing, first positioning himself in front of his disciples, then pacing randomly about in their midst. He now sits down on the boulder behind him so that half of the men are on his right and the other half on his left. When he speaks to them now, he turns his body alternately to the one group and then to the other.

"Do not pour your energies into the accumulation of material things," he tells those on his right, "things that moths and rust, like thieves, will eventually work their ways in to steal from you. No, invest your sweat into accumulating treasures in Heaven where moths and rust do not even exist. Indeed, I say to you, wherever your heart is, there will be your treasure also.

"Let me put this bluntly. No man can serve two masters. If you so much as try, you'll wind up loving the one and hating the other or, the other way around, hating the one and loving the other. It simply cannot be done. You cannot serve God and your material appetites at the same time. Therefore, do not be consumed by such matters as what you'll eat and drink and what you'll wear. That's what pagans are in a dither about. You focus on the Kingdom of God, and everything else will follow as a matter of course."

Jesus pauses momentarily to shift his upper body toward those disciples to his left.

"Oh yes, another thing: Do not judge other people, for the same standard by which you censure others can snap back and bite you," he then goes on to say, the suggestion of a smile now returning to the corners of his lips. "Don't squint, like so, at the grain of sawdust in your brother's eye and miss the timber lodged in your own. Extract the timber, I say, before you even think of going after that grain of sawdust."

This is greeted by another round of laughter from his audience.

"Ask of your Father and you will be given, search and you will find, knock and the door will be opened to you. If any of you is asked by your own dear child for a piece of bread, you aren't going to hand him a chunk of stone, are you? If he requests fish, you aren't going to toss him a viper, are you? Why, of course not! So if, given all your shortcomings, you know how to give good things to your children, you can imagine how much more likely your Heavenly Father is to give good things to his children who ask of him."

With this Jesus breaks from his homily once more to wander off briefly by himself. The disciples chatter among themselves, though saying little that they haven't said before. For the most part they seem confused by some of the things Jesus is now saying but at the same time are totally overwhelmed by his air of authority.

"Treat other people exactly as you would like them to treat you," he tells them upon his return. "Upon this principle, I tell you, hang all of the Law and the Prophets—it is the very heart and soul of human morality."

"Is that then the gate," Thomas asks him, "by which men must enter your kingdom?"

"It is the Kingdom's Golden Rule," he answers him. "The gate by which people must enter is a very narrow one and the pathway to it is exceedingly narrow. There is a very broad thoroughfare out there also, clogged by the great mass of humanity, which leads to a much, much wider gate. The destination of this thoroughfare is, however, disaster and destruction. The hard, narrow pathway and the slender gate that lead to life—only the few will find them.

"But be on the lookout for the pious play actors out there, for they will tell you differently. They're marauding wolves dressed up like sheep. You can tell them by what they produce. You don't get grapes from thorn-bushes or figs from thistles. And you won't be getting the fruits of the Spirit from these charlatans. It's not the people that are forever gushing out the Lord's name that will enter the kingdom of Heaven, but rather those who actually do my Heavenly Father's will."

Jesus pauses to give further opportunity for those with questions to ask them. It is apparent he's already said what he'd led them up the mountain to say. No one speaks up. They have more than enough to ruminate on already.

"All right, then, let me finish with a little analogy," Jesus says, again standing. "Everyone here who listens carefully to what I've been saying and puts it into practice is like a man of vision who builds his house upon a rock. Down come the torrents of rain and up come the floodwaters. The roaring gales batter that house with all their might, but it stands there indestructible. Why? Because it is built upon a rock.

"And everyone who hears my words and ignores them is like a nitwit who builds his house on sand. When the rains pour and the floods rise and the winds beat upon that house, down it will come with a mighty crash!"

Down the Mountain

T HE COMPANY DESCENDS from the mountain late in the afternoon in much the same pattern as they had ascended it earlier—small groups, two and three to a group, gaps between them; Thomas and Matthew walk side by side where the trail allows. Those ahead and behind talk, when they do, in low tones. Any conversation is for those immediately around them. The elation in their voices and on their faces on their way up has given way to thoughtfulness and perplexity; in some case, it seems to Thomas, patent disappointment. The only disciples whose words he can make out distinctly are Simon the Zealot and Judas Iscariot directly ahead of them and those only intermittently.

Iscariot seems to be in state of consternation.

"Not what you expected?" the Zealot asks him.

"Not a word about his kingdom. Not a single word, Simon."

"It was about how the kingdom's subjects are supposed to comport themselves. Does not that imply a kingdom?"

Apparently not hearing this, Judas grumbles on. "Can you imagine all the time up there and not a single thing about his kingdom? Thought he'd tell us what exactly he wants us for, what he's got in mind for each of us to be doing, who's going to be in charge of this and that, things so we can get on with his kingdom's business. No, not a mention of any of that. All I'm coming away with is that he wants us to out-Pharisee the Pharisees."

"The man's an idealist, Judas."

"He singled us out for something. Chose us, did he not? Chose us from of all the chosen people, but for what purpose? What does he want us to do?"

"As you aptly put it yourself, start out by out-Phariseeing the Pharisees."

"And that's not about to happen. You know them. Never a word or action that's not within the boundaries of the Law. If they're even close to offending, they steer wide of it. Nobody out-Pharisees them. No way."

"So far he seems singularly unimpressed by them."

"What I dearly want to know is what our Christ's kingdom is going to be like and what specifically he wants us to do to bring it about and keep it going."

"For that we'll probably have to follow him up another hill some day."

"Is it too much to want to know what you're supposed to do? I'll follow the man wherever he takes me. I just want to know where that is. Where do I fit in? Where do you? Where do the Temple rulers down in Jerusalem fit in? And the biggy: where do the Romans fit in? How does he plan to take them on? Not a word about any of that, not one word. Think he's going to give the nod to the Zealots and Sicarii?"

Simon shakes his head. "Not after his 'Love your enemies' bit up there today. Sounds like a pacifist."

"My thought exactly. Essene?"

"Too talkative, too lively, too bold for that. Likes the crowds too much. Can't see it," says the Zealot. "Sounds like one sometimes, I'll give you that. 'Turn the other cheek, go the second mile, bless those who curse you'—that's his talk though, not theirs."

"Makes you wonder where his kingdom's coming from, doesn't it?"

"Still thinking about it."

"There are practical matters, my friend. The Roman legions aren't about to throw down their spears because we ask them to do so, even if we ask them nicely. They'll throw them all right, but at us. How's he's going to handle them? You were once in the thick of it. You've done battle with the Romans."

"And I have a feeling my fellow conspirators and I went about it in all the wrong ways."

"You mean in nipping them off one by one—mingling in a crowd and cutting a rogue's throat now and then? Somebody's got to stand up to them. He'd have you handing out ripe figs to them."

"You do understand, don't you? In the name of God we killed people, Judas. We actually killed people"

"You think he knows that?"

"He has to, don't you think? Seemed to have known every last one of us before ever meeting us, didn't he? So why did he pick me, Judas? Clandestine warfare was my thing. At first I thought that was what he wanted me for, but it obviously isn't. So why me?"

"Every man here is probably asking himself the same question."

"But no one else with blood on his hands."

All this Thomas and Matthew, only three or four paces behind the duo, overhear. They do not strain to do so, but the Zealot's and Judean's voices are so loud they cannot help but hear every syllable perfectly. Some of their chatter strikes a chord in Thomas and, if Matthew's grimaces are any indication, in the erstwhile publican as well.

As the incline becomes less steep and the path wider, Thomas reaches over to place his hand on his companion's shoulder to suggest they create more space between them and the two ahead of them. Matthew obliges.

"I wouldn't let it worry me," says Thomas, when they're clearly beyond earshot.

"What? Oh, the hidden dagger thing—no, that doesn't faze me, not at all. Honestly. I couldn't have been too high on their kill list, if I was on it at all. This one might have loathed me. Probably did and maybe still does. I was fair in the tax business and gave people breaks when they were desperate. I think they knew that. But what does bother me is that the Judean's got what just happened on the mountain all backwards. Grumbling because he didn't tell us about his kingdom. He did. He began exactly where Moses did twelve hundred years ago."

"How so?"

"By first defining the characters of the chief players," Matthews says. "Moses went up the mountain and unveiled the Law of God. The man we think to be the Christ went up the mountain and unveiled the spirit of that Law. It was only after Moses came down with the tablets well tucked under his arm that he went on to detail the structure of the forthcoming kingdom.."

"First the code then, and after that the commission—that what you're saying?" Thomas wants to know.

"Not immediately, you understand. It'll come, it'll come."

"Something almost familial in how he talked about God. Or didn't you pick up on that?"

"How could one not?"

"Referred to God as his father time and time again. His favorite word for God."

"Not just his father. Ours as well. We're not simply the children of Israel, but of God Himself. I have no idea whether the designation's original with him, but he insisted on it, kept saying it as if we needed it drummed into our heads. A rather lofty standing for the likes of you and me, wouldn't you say?"

"Could be figurative. I took it as metaphor, meaning God's like an ideal father just as, in David's metaphor, He's the ideal shepherd. That's what I thought. He means God's like a father. Conceptually we have no real picture of God. He's beyond us. To ascribe paternalistic qualities to Him may be helpful. To see Him as the ideal father, irrespective of all the real fathers we've known, may be the closest we can get to imagining what God's like. Make sense?"

"Suppose it goes beyond mere metaphor?" Levi Matthew asks.

Thomas doesn't see how it possibly could

"Something to toy with in any event. If so, that would account for his rather fantastically high expectations of us, don't you think? Wants us to turn the world upside down. Fight our own natures tooth and nail. Outdo Moses and outdo the Prophets."

"Definitely wants us to know that the kingdom of God's first and foremost a moral entity."

"Inhabited by the meek, the poor, the bereaved, the persecuted, those with an appetite for righteousness. And us too when we've been persecuted for his sake. Made it sound like regular potpourri of the world's dispossessed. No mention at all of the rich or dignified. Did you not find that strange? Everything topsy-turvy from what we've always thought."

"You think he might have meant all that stuff about the disenfranchised coming out on top was literal, Levi?"

"I see where one can make a case for that. But, even if it were somewhat poetic, is there not truth in the poetry? Did he not portray the constituency of his kingdom as being largely made up of castoffs? Literally or poetically, it comes out the same. In either event he seems to envision an assemblage of the world's most unlikely people."

Thomas consents. "Makes us all look something like a dysfunctional family with God as father."

"A little other worldly to say the least."

"Certainly substantially at odds with the world we've always known."

"More so in my case," Matthew tells him, his voice now suddenly somber and soft to the point of becoming almost inaudible. "Flat out says the pursuit of mammon is at variance with a pursuit of God, which for me makes it very personal. Of that, friend Thomas, I must plead guilty. Of treason, as some accuse me, I protest my innocence. Not so in my gathering of shekels. Moses castigated his generation for worshipping the golden calf. I left off the calf and simply worshipped the gold."

"Few of us, if any, can claim clean hands at that point," Thomas replies.

"And yet he chose us. Do you not find that remarkable?"

"The chosen from among the chosen was the way Iscariot put it. Does not that imply a new trek into a new promised land?"

"Ah yes, the old chosen people theme," says Matthew slowly, as if parsing the syllables as he speaks. "What exactly did 'chosen' used to mean? Did it mean something to be smug about? That's how it often seems—a synonym for 'favorite,' 'special,' 'dearest,' 'coddled,' maybe 'most prized'—right?"

"Is not that roughly what it means?"

"I think we have to ask ourselves, 'For what?' Chosen yes, picked out of the human pack, but for what? What were Abraham's descendents chosen for? To be God's pets? To be singled out by reason of birth to be treated better than anyone else, to be given the choice lambs, the sweetest delicacies, the purest gold and the bluest robes and, of course, a promised land? That is, I think we can agree, the general understanding of it."

Thomas nods, knowing there is more.

'There was an old rabbi I used to know, hard of hearing and very poor eyesight," Matthew tells him, "but wise. A very wise man, this rabbi."

"Yes, I'm sure he was."

"He believed we were chosen *for* something and not just *to* something, that there was a purpose in it all, a mission you might say. We had a calling. God appointed us to do something very important."

"And did your rabbi friend have a view as to what that thing was?"

"To be His envoys to the world at large, his heralds, so to speak, to announce that He alone is the great God Jehovah and there is none other. In Abraham's day and yet in our own, people had many gods, principally fertility deities and sky deities. Our Father in Heaven wanted somebody to tell the world there was one single true god, Jehovah, and that He demanded we live our lives in light of certain basic morals values."

"The Laws of Moses."

"And the principles broadly inferred in them, what Jesus calls the spirit of the Law. He wanted us, the family of Abraham, to be a light to the rest of the world. Such was our assignment. Not to be coddled and pampered, but to get out there and show people who God was and what He wanted of us."

"Ethical monotheism's what I think they call that."

"Whatever the tag, I think my guy was on target."

"And so do I," says Thomas. "Your rabbi friend was a wise fellow indeed."

"All of which makes you wonder what's next," says Matthew. "Now comes the Christ—in our view anyway—and he's chosen twelve of us from the already chosen. For what purpose? Makes you wonder if there's a next step, an extension of some sort perhaps."

"I don't follow."

"With a new ethical standard, why then not a new perception of mission as well? A different kind of kingdom maybe?"

"I don't allow that it is a different ethical standard. The same things that were wrong in Moses' time are wrong today. Nothing's changed in that respect. Moses' Laws are just as applicable as they've always been. In his Golden Rule what Jesus wants us to do is to see the principles behind them, the spirit of them, and apply them directly. A new perspective, yes, but the same code."

"For all practical purposes that amounts to a different ethic, Thomas. It's a higher bar."

"The bar's been there all along. We just didn't look hard enough for it."

"How so?"

"We agree, do we not, that Jesus' new twist to the Law takes his ethics beyond codified behavior into the realm of attitude? He focuses on states of mind—lust, rage, hate, materialism and the like. Sin is not strictly in actions but in the mindset that launches the actions."

"Yes."

"That is not as brand new as one might think. Two of Moses' Ten Commandments have been about states of minds from the very start—to wit, *You shall have no other gods before me* and *You shall not covet.*"

"But you must concede that Jesus' focusing almost exclusively on sins of attitude, states of mind as you call them, is a radical departure from what we've heard all our lives."

"Granted."

"He pointed to love of mammon as worship of a false god, did he not?"

"Yes."

"And covetousness is the very core of our commerce, is it not? The most blatantly righteous among us fantasize sexual escapades, do they not? They desire this man's house and some other fellow's chariot and yet another guy's pasture of sheep. Their heads can be chockful of sin, by Jesus' definitions, but they're upright as long as nobody can see into their heads. Get the tithe right and don't get caught breaking the Sabbath, and you'll be okay. That's the ethical standard we're held to. And Jesus won't have it. In that respect I still say his is a new ethic. He's a revolutionary, and his Golden Rule is the harbinger of great things to come."

"And so you think there might be a revolt somewhere in the making?"

"It's a thought I'm not ruling out at the moment, you might say."

They walk on for a ways with neither speaking.

Ahead of them the Zealot and the Judean are still at it, at points so loudly that Thomas, trying hard not to hear, still cannot help but pick up words now and then. They are clearly not agreeing at all now, occasionally outrightly shouting at each other. Presently Iscariot barges ahead of his companion to leave Simon strolling at slower pace alone.

For the rest of their way down the hillside Thomas and Matthew stroll on in relative silence. There is too much for contemplation, too much to chew on, too much exploding in their heads. Thomas is bowled over by all that he has heard. Tangential chatter can wait.

It is not long before Simon the Zealot, who has chosen to lag well behind the Judean, begins to lumber along, shortening his step until he is about to be overtaken by Thomas and Levi Matthew. As they draw almost even with him, he turns abruptly around directly in front of the latter. Their faces cannot be more than two spans apart.

"We going to be all right?" he wants to know.

Matthew, from all appearance not taken aback by the question, gives him a quick nod. "We are. For my part I'm truly sorry."

"And so am I."

The two men then place their hands on each other's shoulders, each one's eyes fixed on the other's. Thomas cannot read either's looks except, to his relief, they are not about to strangle each other. Something unsaid is going on. Pain, sorrow, relief, and the hint of joy are in their brows and in the lines of the two men's faces as both move yet closer to embrace one another. A stranger passing by would think them brothers, long alien one from the other, estranged and irreconcilable, reunited now in common enterprise.

A miracle, thinks Thomas, a healing of a different species.

Opposition

They have been back in Capernaum for well over a week now and have yet to see any of the theologians or Pharisees within a furlong of them. Thomas thinks this most strange. "They have to know he has a cadre of insiders around him, and there are conjectures everywhere that he might be the Christ," he says to Matthew, the Zealot standing next to him. "You'd think they'd come by again to sound us out, take us on or even join us. Have they no interest in him at all?"

"Their interest is most keen," Matthew answers him.

"Probably got cronies in the crowd. Of that you can be certain," Simon comes in. "And they aren't about to join us. They knew my old comrades also but chose to distance themselves from anything that smelled of revolution."

"He talks of holy living though, not revolution."

"He talks also of his kingdom, and to them that is revolution. My guess is that they get their conclave together every day to figure out what to do about the Nazarene problem. And that's probably how they refer to him. Maybe twice or three times a day."

"They're doubtless biding their time, looking for some occasion to pounce on us," Levi Matthew predicts. "It's only a matter of time."

This conversation takes place early one Sabbath morning. Elsewhere in the homes of Capernaum families are most likely sitting down to eat their simple meals, painstakingly prepared the previous day, before going about the process of dressing for the synagogue later. Jesus' disciples, who have not yet eaten their early meal, are also at breakfast, but for them the meal is made up entirely of wheat kernels they are able to glean from a field just beyond the city gates. And so it is that, as they talk, they pluck heads of ripe wheat, which they roll around in their hands; then, blowing away the chaff, they pop the grains into their mouths. Jesus is there with them, occasionally breaking into their conversations himself.

It has been a most pleasant morning for all of them..

Suddenly they are descended upon by a squadron of Pharisees. The holy men appear on three sides of them and, faster than a pack of feral curs, close quickly around Jesus. Thomas recognizes some of them from their encounter on the evening of Matthew soiree. Hate is in their brows, ambush in their eyes. "Aha," says one of them, bringing his face to within a cubit of the Master's, "your disciples are harvesting grain on the Sabbath, which is in clear violation of the Law of Moses."

"This is breakfast, not a harvest!" Peter, standing just behind Thomas, angrily blurts out.

Jesus holds up his hand to stay his disciple, then addresses their accuser. "They're hungry," he explains, "and need something to eat. That's all."

"Any harvesting of grain on the Sabbath is a violation of the Law!" this overseer of public morality says dogmatically. "You, a rabbi, have to know that."

"What I know is that the Law allows for exigencies," says Jesus. "Do you not remember that passage about what David did when he and his men were hungry? Do you not remember that they went into the Tabernacle and ate the showbread, which only the priests were supposed to eat? There was no hubbub over that."

"But the Law does not allow for the breaking of the Law."

"You abide the priests' working on the Sabbath, don't you?" Jesus says next. "They can break the Sabbath if they're in the Temple, isn't that what you say? Any other place, no. But as long as they are in the Temple, it's okay. The Temple somehow makes some kind of difference. The Law itself makes no such distinction. You people made that up and hold everybody to it."

"It's there by implication."

"Well, I'm telling you there's much more at issue here than the Temple. Do you not remember where the Scriptures say, 'I desire mercy and not sacrifice'? Look it up. Then you'll not be so quick to pass judgment on people who haven't done anything wrong. Man was not made for the Sabbath, but the Sabbath for man!"

The Pharisees and their companions stomp off, albeit but slowly, as though searching for retorts and finding none. Rage registers in their faces, and their grumbling reminds Thomas of thunder as it gradually fades while disappearing into the distance.

"The Sabbath as gift—that's a take I've never heard before," says Matthew afterwards, nodding his head a number of times as if having just made a discovery, "but makes sense."

Thomas and Simon think so too.

Once their company has left the scene, Jesus and his entourage go back to finishing their meal and then at leisure head for the synagogue, where it so happens that Jesus is to be rabbi of the day. He does not tell them this, though, until they are about to enter. They part at the doorway, Jesus himself advancing to the podium and his disciples to the benches. Thomas looks about him as he and his companions seat themselves near the rear of the building where scattered spaces are available. To either side and directly in front of him are men whose faces he knows, having seen then in the wheat field earlier that morning. They look no happier now that they did then, although the thunder has appreciably died down.

Presently there is a commotion of some sort at the very front of the room. Thomas cannot discern the character of it, nor by their looks apparently can the Pharisees and theologians about him either. They sit forward on their benches and crane their necks this way and that, some half-rising in place, but settle back in patent bewilderment.

The Pharisee right beside Thomas slowly stands up as if to adjust his robe beneath him and then, robe attended to, sits down again. "The gimp with the freaky hand," he whispers to the Pharisee on the other side of him.

"Will he . . . on the Sabbath?" his fellow asks.

In hushed tones the information is quickly passed down to the others of their ilk. Thomas hears hints of thunder again, this time initially faint as though from a remote distance, muffled rumbling gradually building as the word is passed on and then, with all the Pharisees and theologians fully informed, breaking into brisk animal noises—cacklings, grunts, growls, and roars reverberating throughout the place of worship.

At the front stands Jesus, composed and perfectly calm. He presently nods to someone close to the front. "Stand," he tells whoever it is, motioning now with his hand, "and come up here."

The man does as he is told. Everyone in the building can now see the fellow's right hand. It is absolutely ghastly, so shriveled and twisted that one would not recognize it as a human hand at all. The men immediately around him are turned so they don't have look at it.

The Pharisees at Thomas's side springs quickly to his feet.

"Hold it there!" he shouts out. "Do not do what you're about to! This is the Sabbath. Is it right to heal anyone on the Sabbath day?"

"You tell me," says Jesus calmly looking up in their direction. There is no trace at all of antagonism in his voice. "Should one do good on the Sabbath day or harm? Which is it? Or let me put it this way: If any of you or any of your fellows had a sheep that stumbled into a deep ditch on the Sabbath, would he not get down there to grab hold of the animal and hoist it out?"

He pauses for an answer, but there is none.

Then matter-of-factly he asks, "Is not a man more valuable than a sheep?"

The Pharisee slowly sits back down. He does not utter another word. Nor does anyone else.

Stillness comes over the congregation as Jesus turns once more to the wretch with the ugly hand and says, "Reach forth your hand."

The man obeys, and a miracle is performed before their very eyes. His hand immediately becomes as whole as anyone else's in the synagogue. The people gasp in amazement. All eyes are fixed on the beneficiary of Jesus' extraordinary powers. But the Pharisees around Thomas do not seem thrilled at all. They harrumph in unison and file hurriedly out of the building.

The people give little notice to their noisy demonstration.

Everyone is amazed, though no one more than Thomas. A

genuine miracle! And he's just witnessed it himself firsthand. Not that he needs it any more than any of his fellows. Seeing with own eyes the nature-defying powers of Jesus is, nevertheless, he has to own, one of the most exhilarating and satisfying moments of his life. He cannot take his eyes from the once-shriveled hand. It's as sound and whole as any of theirs.

Did not the Pharisees also witness it? he wonders. *Did they not see the very same thing I did? If so, how could they flee from the synagogue as if the place were on fire? It does not make sense.* He shakes his head over and over again.

It is only later that he raises these questions with Levi Matthew.

"Tell me, if you know, why they were so angry," he added. "They were livid, frothing from their mouths almost—those around me anyway. You'd have thought he'd quartered their wives and children."

"He cut them off at their knees," Matthew tells him, "or worse."

"How so?"

"By encroaching on their territory. They see themselves as God's official authorities in the interpretation of Mosaic Law."

"How much interpretation is required for something that's as obvious as the nose on your face to begin with? Don't work on the seventh day or require anyone else to work—seems simple enough"

"What constitutes leisure and what constitutes work? They've a virtual catalogue on that," Matthew tells him. "And another catalogue on exceptions: feeding livestock, household emergencies, what's allowed if the ram gets loose or lightning strikes the barn or there's a sudden freeze, and how far can you walk before the heavy breathing sets in. They try to define every possible exigency."

"All that seems a bit arbitrary."

"Oh, it most certainly is. And they've got another catalogue on what constitutes a tithe."

"Not only arbitrary but presumptuous. They're adding to Moses, supplying details he might never have intended to be there. Adding to Moses and passing it all off as, 'Thus says the Lord.' Very presumptuous I'd say"

"I agree, but that's why they see Jesus trespassing on their territory. He's effectively telling them it isn't theirs after all. They've always treated it as their own private domain, and he's saying it isn't even theirs in the first place."

"So he's announcing to the world they're all wet."

"Essentially that, yes," the former publican agrees. "He's unmasking them."

"Let me get this straight. The theologians have done the calculations, and the Pharisees have essentially endorsed them. Is that it?"

Matthew nods his head.

"So it wasn't just righteous indignation I heard raising a roar all around me. It was Jesus' calling their game."

"An anthill of righteous indignation no doubt, I would say, but a mountain of chagrin at having their little game exposed for what it is. All this while they've been lying in wait for him, ready to pounce. They needed to discredit him, publicly if possible. Catch him offending at some point where the Law is exact."

"Their take on the Law, but not necessarily Moses'"

"They treat them as one and the same."

"So twice they pounced on him and thought they nailed him, and twice as quick as a flash Jesus cited the Scriptures that basically said hunger trumps custom and so does mercy. End of argument. No rebuttal."

"And you could almost see the steam coming from their nostrils both times."

"And the second time, you had to have noticed, there was more than a hint of anger in his own voice."

"Okay, there's something I still don't get," Thomas tells the publican. "In plain sight of everybody there he heals this pathetic guy. Tells him to reach out his arm. And he does, and, presto chango, before you can blink, his arm becomes a normal arm. I feel like hollering out, 'Hallelujah!' It's the most amazing thing I've ever seen. I knew he could heal. But something like that, when it happens, is absolutely incredible!"

"That it is," Matthew agrees.

"And so, I ask you again, did not the Pharisees and theologians around me see it too? Why did they not leap to their feet a cry 'Hallejulah' with me? Have they no eyes? Why did they storm out? They acted as though what happened didn't happen at all. That makes no sense."

Matthew tells him he is right. It does not make sense.

"But things have to make sense," insists Thomas.

"We have to get used to the idea that sense may no longer be in vogue and quite possibly desperation is. Jesus has effectively told these spiritual icons of our community that they are no longer needed because the vocation they've been pursuing their whole lives is superfluous. And on top of that, he's basically told them they never understood the whole Sabbath idea in the first place. A lot for them to swallow, you have to realize."

Beyond Galilee

T HE IDEA THAT Simon the Zealot might have been an assassin (and not too long ago) haunts Thomas when he lies down to sleep at night. Although Matthew, contrary to the tax-collector's own best guess, might indeed have barely escaped the young man's knife and is now one of the former cutthroat's closest companions, the thought of bedding down under the same roof as a warrior of any kind, though befriended by a possible victim, is disquieting. He finds, however, that Levi Matthew's company often entails Simon's as well. The fellow has a good head, though, and so it is that he gradually warms to him—in fact, comes to like him a great deal.

But of all the men in Jesus' train it is Judas Iscariot, the lone Judean, he has the hardest time trying to figure out. The fishermen, by profession optimists, are generally pleasant to be around. They're by no measure men of the world, but Jesus is now their only agenda and they cling to his every word and seem thoroughly occupied in trailing after him to facilitate his mission wherever he chooses to go. They're understandably in the fog much of the time. But so is he. And, for that matter, so is Matthew.

Philip and Nathanael are another pair of you-get-exactly-what-you-see types, a little more mellow than the fishers but fully as earnest and accommodating. Although outspokenly perplexed by questions Thomas asks and things he says, good fellows to be around. The other two, a second James and a second Judas, are of much the same stripe, both registering due amazement at all Jesus does and says.

Iscariot is still enigmatic though. He's pleasant enough, yes, but in ways merchants and other panderers are pleasant. You're never sure what's going on in his mind. There's nothing glaringly obsequious or toady about the man. It's a combination of small things—slight edges in his voice, hints of grimace, his eyes drifting up or away when he disagrees with something or downcast when someone disagrees with him, his habit of busily adjusting his robe about him whenever anyone takes time to ponder an action he apparently thinks is automatic. Nuances merely but, to Thomas, nuances with tongues of their own.

When they're on the road, as they are now, Iscariot is always right up there beside Jesus, ever the able lieutenant, standing tall, briskly in step every bit of the way, at the Master's beck every instant, spritely sprinting this way and that when told to do something, already viceroy-in-chief. What little money the company has is in a pouch attached to Judas' belt. He carries himself with a slight air of importance.

And the Zealot is still the Judean's closest friend, maybe his only real friend, in their ranks. So it is that whatever Thomas learns of the Judean's perspectives, such as that Iscariot is not ready to give up on the Pharisees just yet and still speculates about possible roles for them in Jesus' upcoming kingdom, is almost always hearsay. Most recent has been Judas' theory about Jesus' choosing exactly twelve disciples.

"Thinks we might all be from different tribes and the Master plans for each of us to rule over his own historic tribe," Simon tells Thomas.

"Interesting theory," Thomas replies, "but what about the fact that we have two sets of brothers?"

"Exactly the question I asked him."

"And how did he answer?"

"He pointed out that the first generation sons of Israel lived fourteen hundred years ago, and so by now we each have the bloodlines of six or eight, maybe all twelve tribes."

"But, if we turn out to be as mongrelized as he suggests, would it not be impossible to divide up the country by tribe? How would we know how much of a given tribe is in any of us? The original boundaries, which the Romans have completely redrawn, aren't clear anymore, except that eight and a half of the tribes were up here, two and a half on the other side of the river, one down there and the other all over the place. The only sure thing with a scheme like that is that Iscariot himself would wind up governor of Judah. The notion seems to be a little self-serving."

"Just a wild hair—no doubt joking when he said it."

"A bit grandiose, I'd say, even if a put-on. Does it not cross the man's mind that our roles might be those of attendants and errand runners?"

"If it has, he's not letting on," Simon replies.

They have been roaming the length and breadth of Galilee for the better part of a fortnight now, for the most part into hamlets and villages of Capernaum's hinterland that Thomas has never visited before. Whether their keeping to outlying areas has anything to do with trying to evade Roman cohorts in the event of a sudden sweep of malcontents he himself does not know. Some of the men suggest that, but there is no confirmation of their suspicions by Jesus. He preaches, tells parables, and heals as he did in the city.

After his conversation with Simon the Zealot, Thomas, variously motivated, has made a point of trying to get closer to Judas Iscariot. He is up there with Jesus too now, keeping stride with Judas, though a step or two directly behind him, as they move from thinly populated areas to more urban centers. His conversations with Iscariot are sporadic and brief for the most part.

"You see his strategy, don't you?" the Judean asks him at one point as the two are shoulder to shoulder.

"What strategy?" Thomas sees only a lengthy walk and an occasional breaking into a trot.

"It isn't that people out here haven't heard of Jesus," Iscariot explains. "They have, but what they need is to hear and see him up close. Witness his wonders firsthand in their own backyards, you understand, get his image fixed in their minds—so when he finally says, 'March!' they'll already be on their toes to take off in an instant."

"He's going to do that, you think? Say, 'March'?"

"When the day comes—next week, a month, maybe a year from now. It's going to be a mass movement. It has to be. Some of us have been talking about how he's going to take on the Romans. Well, he isn't. That's the conclusion I've come to. I've given it a lot of thought. It isn't his style. Not at all. No pitch battles on the horizons. None. Only other thing's a mass movement, the size and likes of which the world's never seen. Simon agrees with me. Ask him sometime. The Master gives his signal and out they come, every last one of them, from their fields and kiosks and fishing boats, from their kitchens and the meadows where they watch their sheep. From Dan to Beersheba they'll stream, I'm telling you, thicker than those locusts Moses called down upon Pharaoh's fields. In the thousands and the tens of thousand they'll descend on the Holy City to shout their hosannas to their king."

"I love your scenario, Judas. But how can you be sure that the Romans, who have no hosannas in them, will not fall into phalanxes at all eleven of Jerusalem's gates to deter them?"

"The details I leave to him. Just don't be surprised if it happens roughly as I said, for there is no other strategy whereby he can claim his kingdom. None. I have thought long and hard about it."

"Do you see the Herodians and Sadducees and Pharisees all falling in behind him?"

"When the time comes, I think they'll be swept up like everybody else."

Thomas chooses not to argue. It is enough that he encounters the most politic of his fellows on one of his rare upbeat days. He is not about to cast a pall over any man's dream. It sounds to him as though maybe some of Simon the Zealot's fantasy life has gotten to the Judean. If so, then let it be.

But has Jesus himself said a word so far that would warrant such a conclusion? Could a crowd by its sheer mass intimidate the conquerors of the whole world? Or would an army whose trade is butchery not go ahead and butcher a few thousand more to maintain its much vaunted Pax Romana?

Such questions whirl in Thomas's mind but he gives no voice to them. Twice, however, in their trek about Galilee he does ponder the Judean's grandiose scenario when he witnesses his reactions to two of Jesus' acts of healing.

The first comes the very next day when he sees a throng awaiting them as they approach a particularly large village. Thomas, normally more a lover of solitude than gregariousness, has been uncharacteristically warmed by the sounds and sights of crowds on this tour abroad. Time was when huge mobs challenged his belief in a caring God. Masses of people seemed little different from masses of cattle or sheep or swine, even little different from maggots layered on carrion. The bigger and tighter the crowds, the less human they seemed, the less individual, the less capable of being persons that the great God Almighty might individually peer down upon with love. Mobs, not philosophers, were to him the mid-wives of disbelief. Why he is now heartened by the crowds that Jesus draws he does not know, nor does he see need to ask why. He just is.

So it is that he feels warmth as they advance on this assemblage.

Until they are almost upon them they seem like other such crowds, but soon he sees this is not so. Emerging from their ranks are a group of older men, by dress and demeanor dignitaries of some sort, threading their ways to the fore. The other people seem to recognize them and open their ranks to let them through.

"Master, have mercy," pleads their spokesman, kneeling at Jesus' feet.

"Is one of you ill?" he asks. "You all seem to be whole."

"Not for ourselves but for someone else we seek your mercy. The man of whom I speak is, in fact, a slave. Even as we stand here, he is deathly sick. He belongs to a Roman centurion, who has time and again proven his goodwill and affection for this place. Out of the generosity of his heart he built us our synagogue with his own money. He's the one who has asked us to come to you for help."

It is at this point that Judas, stern in countenance and clearly upset, begins to step forward to respond in Jesus' stead, but Jesus smoothly blocks him from doing so and nods to the group's spokesman to lead him to the centurion's house, which forthwith he does. Jesus follows quickly on the man's heels, and his disciples after him with the crowd not far behind them. Murmurs rise up from the crowd. They sound like a swarm of hyperactive honeybees.

As they all head up the pathway to the centurion's house, they are met by a number of the centurion's friends. Speaking for the Roman, one of the men steps forward to say, "My master thought himself unworthy to come to you in person, good sir, as even now he feels it humiliating for you to come beneath his Gentile roof. Just give the order and make his beloved slave well. That's all he asks. He too is used to giving orders, saying to this one, 'Go,' and he goes, or to another, 'Come,' and he comes, or to still another, 'Do this,' and he does it."

"Now that is what I call real faith!" Jesus turns to tell the crowd behind him. "So far I have not found faith of this magnitude—no, not in all of Israel."

Out of the corner of his eye Thomas sees Iscariot cast his gaze downward, contorting his face as though something is amiss, then glance quickly over to Simon the Zealot, apparently seeking support in whatever seems to be bothering him.

The Zealot frowns ever so slightly in response.

Jesus stops short and then to the centurion's envoy says, "It is done."

Those who came outside from the centurion's house now rush back into it. Presently the crowd on the pathway can hear whoops of rejoicing from within: "Amens!" and "Hallelujahs!" and "Praises be to God, he's whole!" The loudest, most excited voice is that of someone used to giving orders.

"He's opening the door now to the Romans," says Iscariot.

"The teeniest crack at the most, I'd say," Thomas responds. "We know nothing of the man he healed. Probably one of our own."

That Jesus has now healed someone by proxy goes unnoticed by his disciples. They just seem to assume now that he will heal whomever he wants to and however he wishes to do it. Healings to them have become as common as goodwives calling their families to the dinner table. Why would this one then upset anyone in the train? Judas's perturbation lasts throughout the rest of that day well into the next. He seems for some reason downright offended by it.

The second instant occurs some days later just outside of a very small village called Nain to the east and south of Nazareth. As they approach the gates to this hamlet, a funeral procession is coming out. The corpse on the litter, but a youth, is being carried by four pallbearers. A lone woman, bent and broken by grief, weeping uncontrollably, follows close behind and behind her four or five other mourners.

"She's a widow," explains a woman in the cortege to Jesus. "This was her only son."

Visibly moved by this, Jesus approaches the bereaved mother.

"Do not cry," he says softly to her and thereupon walks over to the bier and, while the bearers stand in place, reaches out his hand to place it near the dead boy's head.

"Wake up, young man!" he commands.

By now several of Jesus' disciples have positioned themselves around the corpse, stone-still also, none so much as blinking. They gasp in unison as the boy's fingers seem to twitch. Then his eyelids break open enough so that they can see a thin slit of his eyeballs; then all the way. The deathly glaze that covered them quickly disappears. He then blinks, as also do most of the onlookers. Soon he shifts his body in place to sit up. Then, as the pallbearers continue to hold his bier at knee level, he brings his legs around to the side so that his feet are firmly planted on the ground. He looks briefly around and begins to talk as though just awakened from a sleep.

Jesus takes the man's hand and places it in his mother's. "Your son, my dear woman," he says kindly, and soon all are on their way again.

The disciples, inveterate watchers of run-of-the-mill healing, are aghast by this episode. They glance in such amazement at each other one might think the earth itself had just stopped.

"He couldn't have really been dead," says one man.

"Hard to say," Thomas theorizes. "People do go into deathlike states—the Greeks have a name for it. I forget what it is. At any rate, they've been buried alive and then subsequently clawed themselves out of their graves. Maybe that's the case here. He did say, 'Wake up.'"

"Looked awfully dead to me," ventures someone else.

Once on their way again, Iscariot, one of the two or three disciples who were not at bierside, snarls to Thomas, "It's immaterial as to whether the boy was actually dead or not. Don't they see that?"

"What is material then, pray tell?"

"Timing."

"How so?"

"Hardly a soul around," Judas laments. "His mother, a handful of family. That's all. It was a waste. If he's going to raise people from the dead, you'd think he'd want to have a good crowd on hand. Do it in Jerusalem maybe or at least in a place like Capernaum. Out here in the bush who's ever going to know?"

Thomas does not respond.

Nor does the Judean pursue the matter further beyond mumbling, mostly to himself and no one else in particular, that it is probably virtually impossible for Jesus not to heal whenever asked to do so. "Has to do it. Just can't help himself. But timing's crucial. Doesn't seem to have much of a head for timing."

For days they continue to roam the countryside, and everywhere it is the same. Whenever invalids can drag themselves to Jesus or be hauled there by friends, he halts everything to heal them. One day it's a blind man, the next a deaf woman, and the following morning a paralytic and then a dumb man. Everywhere the same. With but a word he stretches new skin over lepers' arms and then goes on to free epileptics from the demons within them. People wan with fevers are brought to him in litters and leave walking upright in the pink of health.

Iscariot perks up. No longer moody. He's chipper for longer stretches of time; the jaunt is back in his stride, all smiles, steeped in good cheer. There are times, though, when Thomas still wonders. One such instance comes right after Jesus heals a man of a congenital deformity and the crowd about them is agape in amazement as the fellow skips down the path away from them.

"Can say one thing about him," says Judas. "Sure knows how to get the masses behind him."

"Getting the masses behind him? That isn't why he does it," John quickly objects.

"Then why does he?"

"Don't you see the compassion in his eyes? He loves them. His heart goes out to them."

"What's there to love in the likes of some of them?" says the Judean, with a hearty snicker.

"Loves them for themselves. They believe in him, and that's what he most wants. Faith. You've heard him say it dozens of times. These poor broken wretches believe he can do wonders for them. So he does. I think it's that simple."

"But he's a king in the making, not a physician," Iscariot shoots back. "His work is ultimately to heal the land, not its endless legions of beggars. He needs right now to put his name on every tongue in Israel. Which is exactly what he's doing."

"Compassion and that only," again insists John.

"The suffering and the insufferable, like the poor, we will have with us always," counters Judas, not about to let it go. "Here our whole nation groans out for deliverance. I'd prefer that he bring in his kingdom first and then attend to the aches and pains of this one and that, but, I concede, he must first get their attention."

The matter is soon dropped as they set out toward yet another Galilean village.

Jesus' reputation is being spread rapidly throughout the whole region: north into the Gentile realms of Tyre and Sidon, east into Decapolis on the other side of the Jordan, and south through Samaria and Judea as far as Idumenia. Travelers from all parts, strangers with strange dialects, are showing up almost daily in the open country and at the fish markets in towns along the shores of Gennesaret and wherever else Jesus is rumored to be.

The crowds are getting bigger and bigger.

"Why do I feel it in my bones that we'll be heading down to Jerusalem any day now?" Iscariot asks Thomas one morning. "Traders on their way through are saying he's the talk of the city. Time, I would think, he should probably show himself."

"If they're talking about him, you can be sure the Temple crowd is up in arms."

"Maybe literally so. All the more important he oblige them."

By late afternoon Thomas is wondering if there might be something of the prophet in the Judean after all, for it is this very day Jesus tells them that Jerusalem is indeed their next destination. Whether or not this announcement is related to a surprise visit by two of John the Baptizer's disciples earlier at midday is unclear. Some of the men see a direct connection, others none at all.

What happened earlier that day, at noontide, was another cause of grumbling on Iscariot's part, though Thomas saw no reason for such a reaction. They glanced over their shoulders to see four men running toward them from some distance away. No one at first could make out who they were, but Jesus, as though knowing who they were and what their mission was, called a halt so they could catch up. Both looked weary from their travel. They had no doubt been on the road throughout the night.

"A word with you! A word with you!" both called out as they advanced. There was a clear ring of urgency in their voices.

John, Andrew, and Philip, having spent time with the Baptizer, seemed to recognize them right away once they came into clear view. So also, Thomas surmised for reasons unknown, did Jesus himself. He stepped forward to greet them.

"We've come from the Baptizer," they told him.

"And why with such haste?"

"His time's short, and he wants to know if you're the one who is to come or if we should wait for another. He's most anxious to know this before Herod has him killed."

Jesus' disciples leaned in to hear their master's answer.

"Go back and tell John what you yourselves have seen and heard," Jesus told them. "The blind have recovered their sight, paralytics are once more prancing about, lepers are being cleansed, the deaf are made to hear, dead men are being brought back to life again, and the good news is being spread to those in need. Yes, and add this: Blessed is the man who never loses his faith in me."

The men soon turned and, quickly breaking into a run, retreated by the route they'd come.

Whereupon Jesus, patently moved by what the men had told him, looked up at his own men and the crowd about them. "What did the hordes go out in the deserted places to see?" he asked them. "A prophet? Oh yes, most definitely a prophet—and much more than a prophet! This was a man foretold by the Prophets. Trust me, no man greater than John the Baptizer has ever been born. None! But I tell you a humble member of the Kingdom of God is of greater stature than he."

"Why didn't he come right out and tell them who he is?" Judas Iscariot later asks.

"An affirmative answer was implicit in his recitations of proofs," Thomas tells him. "And from the looks on their faces I'd say these fellows took it that way. Would he have gone into all that detail if he'd wanted to keep them guessing, do you think?"

"Why does he always have to be so coy? Could he not just say it."

It is only hours later that their trip to the Holy City is first mentioned and Judas' spirits suddenly shoot skyward once more. "Been right around the corner all the time," he says to Thomas. "Didn't I tell you so?"

Thomas has to concede he did.

"Someday he'll be enthroned there. Only makes sense he'd go down and check it out, doesn't it?" the Judean adds, as if he himself had somehow been party to Jesus' decision.

To Jerusalem and Back

I SCARIOT WILL LATER tell Thomas and the Zealot that their first
excursion into Jerusalem was a reconnaissance trip. "A little jaunt
to discern the lay of the land" is the way he'll put it, saying that
whatever reputation Jesus was to enjoy in the city was the one that
existed when he arrived there, which turned out to be one of no
small character; however, he intended to do nothing to enhance or
diminish it.

"He did not kick the hornets' nests, nor did the hornets swarm
out to sting him," he told his fellows, as though appointed to be
their chief tour guide, "but from safe distances both we and the
Temple insiders did take each other's measures. That was the plan
from the beginning."

And such had roughly been the case.

Apart from Jesus' dialogue with a young Pharisee one night,
neither he nor his party had any discourse with the ruling elite of
the Holy City. There were no confrontations, verbal or physical.
They were safe in the thick of the crowd each day and safely
secreted away each night. Iscariot, who now carried the bag and
saw to all transactions in the company's behalf, saw to that. He,
more than anyone else, knew his way around the city.

Although his officiousness at times bordered on the unbearable,
for once Thomas was comforted by the Judean's presence
among them.

Throughout their entire time in David's city Jesus neither said
nor did anything particularly controversial that would provoke the
Sanhedrin, and they in turn steered wide of him—far enough not
to antagonize in anyway but close enough to hear. Their guard

dogs sniffed at closer range but stayed at bay. It was as though, by truce, each faction was there to size up the other but not to engage.

Each day the crowd was larger than it was the day before. Jesus told stories engagingly and energetically, talked occasionally in riddles, and spoke vaguely of the Kingdom of God. But such activities did not, to Thomas's mind, account fully for Jesus' growing audiences. The stories about him, rumors of who he was—shared with friends in the marketplace, no doubt, discussed in homes at mealtime, and even whispered in the Temple—were what brought the masses. The Temple rulers had to know it too but held back for the time being.

His encounter with the young Pharisee around dusk one evening was prearranged. "You can tell right away he is a novice, not one of the seasoned ilk at all," Judas told his fellow disciples, although he had never met the man. "Polite, mannered and nonjudgmental, he wants to talk with the Master for no purpose other than to learn from him."

"Learn what?" Thomas wanted to know...

"Obviously to ask him if he's the Christ and things about his kingdom."

"Could just as well be to inquire about the Baptizer, couldn't it? Or ask him if he had a good trip? Might want to know how he got through Samaria unscathed. It's all just anyone's guess, isn't it?

"Their meeting was hush-hush," Iscariot, apparently not listening, went on. "I'd say the young fellow's probably worried, as he certainly has cause to be, about reprisals if his fellows learn of it. Some of them are, as the Baptizer himself called them, a nest of vipers. You don't know them like I do. Some are commendable, some as fiendish as old Satan himself."

"Satan's no more than a tester," Thomas told him, "and I doubt if he's even a person, but rather a devil's advocate figure, an objectification of the predilections and doubt that lie within all of us. Consult *Job* someday."

"He's right," Matthew says.

"Be that as it may," Judas retorted. "Some of these Pharisees down here are guys to stay clear of. I can tell you that much."

The truth is that none of Jesus' disciples was party to the secret session Jesus set up with the curious young Pharisee, whose name he later tells them is Nicodemus. Judas Iscariot did volunteer to accompany Jesus, but he politely declined. He wanted to meet the man alone as requested. And when he returned to the house that evening where they were staying, he told them nothing of what transpired. No one pressed him.

Judas was just glad, he said, that he got back safe and sound.

The disciples breathe a collective sigh of relief now when, on their homeward journey, they cross from Judea into Samaria. They are a safe distance from the clutches of the Temple rulers and, equally comforting, from other men of their spiritual hierarchy.

It is not until they are two full days out of Jerusalem that, in bits and pieces, Jesus makes them privy to the conversation that passed between himself and Nicodemus on the night in question. It turns out that, yes, the young Pharisee did indeed want to know about Jesus' kingdom. That, at any rate, was where their conversation quickly drifted.

Satisfaction is suddenly writ large all across Iscariot's face: *Told you so. I was right, wasn't I?* He develops an itch on the back of his neck and is compelled to turn his head slowly around to get to it.

Jesus apparently told Nicodemus right off that the entry requirement to his kingdom was rebirth. "Except a man be born again," he said, "he cannot enter the kingdom of God." And poor Nicodemus, a Pharisee in good standing, could not figure out what he was talking about. That was about the sum of it. They talked mostly about that, but the young man seemed to be in a fog.

"Have to admit, I'm in that same fog," Matthew tells Thomas and Simon later.

"And I'm not quit sure what 'born again' means either," owns Simon.

"Nor I," says Levi Matthew as well. "Thought and thought about it. Came up empty."

"Could be some rite of passage," suggests Thomas.

Matthew wrinkles his forehead. "There's nothing in the Laws and Prophets about such a thing, not that I know of anyway. Just being born once of the blood of Abraham, Isaac and Jacob got you into the camp of the chosen. Not a whisper of having to do it all over again."

"But if he said it," argues Simon, "doesn't that make it automatically true?"

"Could mean that there's some other kingdom, either out there or about to take shape, other than the historical kingdoms of Israel and Judah," Thomas comes in, "one that supersedes them, one with a different constituency and different entry qualifications."

"But one that a person has to be reborn into."

"No way to reenter your mother's womb to repeat the process— that's for certain. He couldn't have meant it literally."

"Could be baptism like the Baptizer's baptism. Baptism could a be symbol of rebirth."

"If baptism is primarily a symbol," says Thomas, "it would not be the identical same thing it symbolizes. The thing it symbolizes is the point of reference, not the ritual that commemorates it. The rebirth itself has to be a different animal."

"The Baptizer's baptism was tied to repentance," Matthew then says.

"With the Baptizer the operative thing was the repentance itself, not a subsequent symbolic act. I think Jesus might be on the same track but is going beyond it somehow. Repentance, yes maybe, but something more."

"He's heavy on faith," says Simon. "Could it somehow be tied to that?"

"Probably is," replies Thomas. "Which begs the question, in turn: How does a person go about acquiring faith? Do you somehow choose it? If so, how? Or is it something conferred upon you maybe? Or does it mysteriously just happen?"

"Or is it the product of reasoning?"

"Say rebirth is a metaphor, which I agree it probably is, and faith is the route you have to take to become reborn," says Matthew, getting back into the conversation, "might there not be any number of roads and byways leading to that destination? Might not happenstance, reason, and choice and all come into play?"

"Sounds plausible," Thomas responds.

Simon the Zealot thinks that's an acceptable premise for the time being and hopes that Jesus will give them more to go on as time passes. "But you wonder about the faith he keeps bringing up," he adds. "Faith in what? God? The Prophets? Him personally? What? Faith itself? It has to be faith in something."

"And when you have it, how do you know you do?" says Thomas.

"The fruit of faith is action," Matthew tells him later. "This wise old rabbi friend of mine once said, 'A person believes something only when he behaves as though it were true.' A very, very wise man, that one. Made a world of sense when I first heard it. Still does."

"There are things," Thomas says after much pondering, "I'm beginning to suspect, that are mysteries we might just have to live with. Thinking might not get us there. They're too big or too opaque or maybe just too simple to get our minds around. Jesus may sit down tomorrow and tell us exactly what 'born again' means and what kingdom he's talking about and how to go about getting faith. And then again he may never explain to our satisfactions any one of them. They might always be mysteries to us. Doesn't mean they aren't important or aren't true, just that we plain don't get them and maybe aren't supposed to."

They are approaching Jacob's Well the morning this particular conversation takes place, not far from the Samaritan village of Sychar. The well is a revered landmark in that region largely because their patriarch himself dug it by hand before awarding it and the land thereabouts to his beloved son Joseph, a site travelers often go out of their ways to visit when passing from Judea into Galilee. Jesus and his company arrive there shortly before midday.

Most of them have seen the well before, even the Master himself, who says he saw it as a boy when he traveled with his family to Jerusalem for the Passover. There was water at its bottom then as there is now. People from the region still come there to fill their water jugs on a daily basis. There is no one there, however, when they come upon the place.

"The respectable women come early before the heat of the day," explains Judas, "the women of disrepute, to avoid the traffic so to speak, at less crowded times." He smirks as if he's told a good one.

None of his fellows responds to this. Jesus, apparently preoccupied with something else, does not seem even to hear it.

"Should go into town and shore up our supplies," Iscariot says next, voice and facial lines now suddenly all business. "Low on lots of things. Be getting pretty hungry by this time tomorrow if we don't."

Jesus consents to this suggestion.

"We all going?"

Only Judas himself and the others to help carry things Jesus tells him. He himself wants stay behind. He does not give a reason for this, but there is something in the way he says it that suggests he does have something in mind. Maybe to pray, thinks Thomas. He does go off by himself to do that, sometimes for the better part of a night. But when he does there's always a somber aspect about his features as though he is especially burdened by something, which isn't the case now. If anything, the air about him this time is one of expectation. But one never knows.

So off the twelve disciples traipse to the markets of Sychar, leaving Jesus seated beneath a tree with his back against the trunk facing the rim of the well only cubits away. Thomas glances at him over his shoulder as they commence their walk townward. It's obvious he doesn't plan to go anywhere.

At the kiosks along the roadway through community's agora and the several alleys just off it they find the sacks of meal, dried and fresh fruits, beans and lentil seeds, cheeses and bread they have need of, skipping the dried sheatfish and barbel. "Probably left over from some we sold them a year ago by the looks," says Peter as they pass by the barrels.

All help with picking out and lugging the goods, but it is Judas Iscariot who, carrying the bag, deals with the various merchants. He's a veteran haggler, you can tell, as also are the fishers in their number. A way of life, the way business is done. Thomas knows that but is still uncomfortable in the midst of it. It involves posturing, for which he has no stomach.

"Not much for this kind of thing," he tells Matthew as he works his way to the back.

"Nor am I either," his friend says, staying with him." I used to tell them exactly what they owed, no more, and that's what they gave me. End of transaction."

"One charges too much, the other offers too little. They haggle, conman against conman, meet in the middle somewhere. A game, no more. Fair trading for everybody except the poor chump that doesn't have the nerve or know-how to play it."

"Maybe why he stayed back—didn't want to witness it."

Thomas shakes his head. "No, I suspect that was for some other reason, although I don't know what."

Having made their purchases, the twelve men start their trek back towards Jacob's Well to rejoin Jesus. They are in good spirits, the Judean in particular because, at his haggling best, he has acquired everything they had need of and, as he puts it, enough shekels left in the bag "to rattle around like a bucket of nails." The legendary King Midas could not have been happier. He was the right person to carry the bag all right. They all had to know that.

They are halfway back to the well when Peter, in the lead, calls their attention to a strange figure hastening directly toward them. It is a woman, trying to run and at the same time balance a water jug on her head. As they advance, so also does she, seeming to up her speed the closer she gets to them.

"I met a man!" she cries out, once in hearing range. "I met a man who knew me, knew all about me before we ever met!"

Thomas realizes in an instant who this man has to be. So do the others. They stop.

Keeping her water jug balanced and in place, she runs the rest of the distance to them and comes to an abrupt halt. There are droplets of sweat on her forehead. Although roughly the same age as most of them, she seems much older. Her arms and face are deeply tanned by the sun, and there are lines along her throat and the beginnings of crow's-feet at the edges of her eyes. The years have definitely not been kind to her. But at the moment her face is aglow and her eyes wide with sheer excitement. She cannot contain herself.

"He was sitting under a tree and rose to his feet when I was lowering the bucket into the well," she explains, talking rapidly so she can get said what she has to say and then hurry on back into the village. "I didn't even see him at first, and then there he was, speaking to me civilly as if I were any other woman, asking me for a drink of water. Nor did he shrink from me or seem to think it strange that I should be there in the heat of the day.

"No one else was in sight. The proper women from the town had already long since drawn their water for the day and were now home, their respectabilities intact, their reputations secure, kneading bread or spinning wool. Assuming the role of intruder, I averted my eyes, as though not knowing he was there, and went about drawing my water.

"'When you draw your pail up, please give me a drink,' he asked again.

"I eyed him carefully. It seemed he'd been waiting for me. And by the light in his eyes and the soft half smile that spread across his face as he stepped closer, I could have almost imagined that, by appointment long ago made and long ago forgotten, he'd been waiting especially for me.

"I was quite frankly startled, for by his dress and dialect I could tell he was a Galilean. And, as you have to know, Galileans do not converse with Samaritans, certainly not with Samaritan women of my stripe. Early in life that was impressed upon me, and never was I allowed to forget it. They think Samaritans renegades, the Jews of both Galilee and Judea. Half-castes we are to them, neither fish nor fowl, with the blood of pagans coursing through their veins, therefore not true Israelites. Like damned Ishmael, my family and friends are to their fellow countrymen baseborn, pollutions of Abraham's pure seed, compromised; like him too, driven out, exiles from that to which we are born, ostracized always from the camp of the chosen. We are the lowest of the low. Galileans and Judeans are both more kindly disposed toward the Romans than toward us, which makes me least among the least.

"'A drink of water,' he asked again.

"No longer pretending I didn't see him, I then turned to face him

"'What is this?' I responded, finally finding my tongue. 'How is it that you, a Galilean, speak to me? Are you not aware that Jews have nothing to do with Samaritans?'

"He shook his head ambiguously. I couldn't tell whether he didn't know what I was talking about or was dismissing it. Neither was the case, it turned out. He was simply ignoring it. 'If only you knew,' he said gently, 'who it is that asks this water from you, you would ask of him and he would give you living water.'

"'Come, come now, sir,' I replied, on the verge of laughing. 'This is a deep well, and you have no bucket. And you're going to give me living water? Pray, how do you intend to go about drawing it?'

"He stepped over to the well and peered for a moment down into it, then, shaking his head again, answered me, 'Whoever drinks the water down there will get thirsty again and again. But not so with my living water. Whoever drinks of that will never be thirsty again. It shall be to that one a veritable fountain gushing forth into eternal life.'

"What water he spoke of I did not know. His voice, nevertheless, was lively and reassuring, engaging my confidence almost immediately. I'd barely met him, yet what he said seemed to strike a chord in me. Suddenly, both mystified and intrigued, I sensed a profound need for what he was offering, although I could not, if required, put a name to it.

"'Oh, sir, I want this water,' I said. 'I know not of what you speak, but do give it to me. Let me drink of it deeply that I might never again be athirst.'

"'Good,' he said to me. 'Go get your husband then and bring him here.'

"'I'm not married,' I told him. 'I have no husband.'

"'That's right, you aren't married, now are you,' he said, his eyes momentarily fixed on mine, seeming somehow to pierce them, penetrate beyond them. As moments earlier he peered into the well, even now for the briefest instant he seemed to be peering into me, searching the secret haunts of my mind for what could never satisfy. 'But you have had five husbands, have you not? And, in fact, you are not married to the man with whom you are now living. Oh yes, my dear lady, when you said you didn't have a husband, you were indeed quite right.'

"He knew me! How I have no idea. But this total stranger with kind eyes knew me right down to the seamy details of my life. I did not know whether I should turn to run or fall on my knees before him. Momentarily frozen in place, I blurted out, 'Oh, sir, I knew it! I knew it from the beginning! You are a prophet indeed!'

"This he did not deny but stared long again into Jacob's Well as if searching for something that wasn't there—to remind me, I think, that the legacy of our fathers is not enough, that there's a thirst in the human soul that water can never quench.

"Then his gaze shifted slowly back to me.

"'Tell me, since you are a prophet, where should we worship?' I unabashedly asked, feeling more comfortable with him, sufficiently relaxed to broach a topic that had long vexed me but which I never dared ask. 'Our fathers worshipped on that mountain over there, but your people say Jerusalem is the only place.'

"'Their god is too small, both your fathers' and my people's,' he told me

"I thought I detected a slight smile tugging at the corners of his lips when he said this, so I cocked my head and raised my eyebrows in search of explanation. 'How so?' I asked.

"'Neither the mountain nor Jerusalem makes a bit of difference, my dear lady,' he explained, 'for God is not of our substance. He is spirit. He is not bound by strictures of time and space. That's what spirit implies. He is everywhere but in no one place in particular. He is vast. God is infinitely vaster than this world. He is vaster than the outer boundaries of the heavens beyond the teeniest flickering star the human eye is able to see.' My words, not his. But that seemed to be the gist of it.

"'I cannot imagine anything like that,' I told him.

"'Nor can anyone else. He is imponderable.'

"Again not in those exact words. That was the idea though."

"'We live and move and have our being in Him. By Him and in Him and through Him have all things been made, and not anything has ever been made without Him. In Him all things consist and have their being, from the endless galaxies about us to the most infinitesimal, invisible components of matter itself.' Something like that anyway."

"'Does this mean that we can never know Him?' I asked.

"'Only as through a very, very mud-besmeared piece of glass,' he told me.

"'My mind, I'm afraid, is too small to comprehend what you are saying.'

"'Let us just say then that God has shown Himself, but only in tiny glimpses, to the prophets and our forefathers. In a brief time His son will show Him as He is, and then the day will come, I assure you, when you will know Him too.'

"I pondered this for a long time before speaking again. Neither the Pharisees of Jerusalem nor the priests at Bethel, I knew, would be conversing with me thus. Considering who I was, they more than likely would not have said a thing. But, if they did, they would certainly not have been trying to go so to the heart of the matter with the likes of me. They would never have talked about God as though such a frail, unschooled sinner could ever really fathom what they said; they would never have dared send me out on my own to worship as he seemed to be doing.

"'Someday,' I said, finally finding my tongue once more, 'the Christ himself is going to come. And he will show us everything about God we need to know.'

"'Look no further, my dearest lady,' he then said, his eyes once more peering deep into mine. 'The person who now speaks to you is he.'

"And, oh, in a flash I knew who he was!

"The scene suddenly made sense. This had to be why I'd said what I did. I had felt it all along. He knew me, knew all about me. Amazing, so incredibly amazing! He knew me like God himself, yet spoke with me as though I were his sister or perhaps his own dear child. I felt a tingling within, a current that coursed through my whole body as though I were transfixed by a bolt of lightning or suddenly cast into euphoric spell by a potent drug.

"Picking up my water jug, I have run as fast as I could to shout the news abroad to my family and friends and the whole world. He knew me. He knew all that ever I did. Is he not the Christ, good sirs? And this day I met him at the well. He asked me, lowliest of handmaidens, for water and gave me his. I must shout it abroad till I can shout no more."

And with that she speeds away, her water jug still in place.

The disciples, in turn, quickly resume their trek back to Jacob's Well to find Jesus.

"We'll find out the real story from him," Iscariot tells Simon the Zealot in the hearing of those about him.

"That I doubt very much. Not the kind of thing he'll likely even mention. And who's to approach him to ask about it? If he wants us to know, he'll bring it up. Otherwise what's there to tell?"

"Has some imagination, I'll give her that."

"To look at her face," Levi Matthew says to Thomas, "you'd think she was born again."

Thomas knows that his friend has to identify with the woman

at the well. "Hope she gets to tell young Nicodemus back in Jerusalem," he turns to tell him. "That would be nice."

Matthew is smiling as broadly as Thomas has ever seen him. "What delicious irony this is. For a solid week, day on end, we trafficked in Jerusalem. There was hardly a moment when members of the Sanhedrin or their underlings were not present in those crowds. They slithered about, but we always knew they were there: our most esteemed citizenry, models of holiness, crème de la crème of the sons of Abraham. But never once did he make formal declaration of himself to them. Then, little more than a day's journey from the Holy City, what does he do? He confides what has to be the most stupendous news in the world to a Samaritan, and a fallen woman that. How like him!"

"Pearls before swine," says Iscariot.

Outsiders In

FROM ALL REPORTS the woman at the well is still bending every ear in Sychar with her account of having met the Christ of God in person. Rumors continue to spread upward into Galilee. It's the talk among the workmen at the marketplace in Capernaum and the fish sellers and buyers and idlers along the northern shore of Gennesaret. On everybody's tongue. Opinions range from utter skepticism to total obsession, the former those of the elite and the latter those of the community's underbelly.

One morning, however, the rumors stop as abruptly as they started. The milk goat, so to speak, goes dry and, put to pasture, is replaced by another. This one is black, though, and its milk bitter, bitter as gall and that to everyone—the dregs and the decorated, the powerful and the powerless, the nabobs and the nobodies, and everybody in between.

For the word is that John the Baptizer has been murdered in his cell. Not trumpeted but whispered, this news evokes grief and fear in all. It is the new talk of all Capernaum, although only a handful of its citizenry ever laid eyes upon the man when he was alive.

He was beheaded a little before dawn, and word of the deed is noised abroad in Galilee before most men have even sat down to breakfast. Late-sleepers are roused from their ticks to be told, and zealous busybodies race to the hovels of the infirm to be the first to let them know. The celebrated woman in Sychar could have drowned in Jacob's well now for all they care.

"The harlot Herodias—Herod's once sister-in-law, now his concubine—was responsible," is, according to one of the early reporters, what people working at Herod's palace are saying.

"Not the king?" asks someone.

"The king himself would probably have let the man sweat it out a few weeks longer and then let him go," the reporter says, "but, no, not Herodias. A real Jezebel that one. She wanted the Baptizer's head on a platter and would have settled for nothing less. You don't shout from the rooftops what she is, you don't say she's no more than a common prostitute, and walk away unscathed. Nosirree, you don't. Got her daughter Salome into it, she did."

No one needs to ask who Salome is. They may never have seen the Baptizer in person, but they've seen the lissome dancing daughter of Herodias, who is rumored to be able to quicken the spirits of old men and even stir new life into the blood of eunuchs. They have heard of her sensuous dancing.

"Dance for the king, my bewitching daughter," Herodias, according to this reporter, told her. "Dance as if for him alone. And when he promises your heart's desire, ask for the head of the Baptizer delivered up on a silver platter."

And so she did.

Herod, enthralled by the dance, vowed to give Salome her heart's desire, just as Herodias knew he would, and she asked for the head of John the Baptizer. The tetrarch immediately repented of his all too hasty promise, but it was too late. Mother and daughter would have their prize. And so that next morning the severed head of the greatest prophet of their time, and maybe all time, was delivered up to the women of Herod's household.

Andrew, John, and Philip are hit hard. For days they talk of little else. The others mourn briefly also, but before long their focus of concern shifts to themselves.

"Could be the beginning of a purge. If they go after him, what about us?" Nathanael wants to know. "The Baptizer was never a threat to Roman rule. We might yet turn out to be."

"Not as long as we pay our taxes and don't call women in high places harlots," says Philip.

"What we're dealing with here," intrudes Thomas, "is perception. And perception is everything. We can be as innocent as lambs; but, if they perceive us to be threats or someone sells them the idea that we are, that's all it'll take. But, if indeed our lives will be required of us, so be it. In the meantime the course of wisdom should be not to stick our necks out unnecessarily."

"Ever the optimist," Judas mutters sotto voce to Simon the Zealot, "although, I dare say, it would be an excellent time for us to scamper some place where we won't be under our king's nose."

When, several days later, Jesus collects his entourage around himself to announce that they will be leaving the lands of Abraham, Isaac, and Jacob and venturing north and west into the region of Tyre and Sidon, Iscariot wonders out loud if maybe something he himself said inspired this precaution. It is a course of action he has heartily espoused.

"Why risk setbacks when all you have to do is sidestep them?" he puts to Thomas and Matthew. "Why jeopardize long-term goals for short-term bravado? Wherever the inspiration for a withdrawal from Galilee came from I personally don't care. Could have been me, could have been one of you. There's sound judgment in it."

Since the Judean carries the bag, there are the practical matters for him now as to what to purchase and what to pick up along the way, details that for the most part are strictly between Jesus and himself. He makes no big thing of it but acts the part of someone in Jesus' inner circle. His opinions are valued.

Thomas, however, does not see this as a strategic retreat at all. The Christ of God is not about to retreat for anything ever. Jesus has never evidenced fear, nor has he ever cautioned them to play it safe. His hide-and-seek maneuvers in Jerusalem were not so much to eschew physical harm as they were to dodge distractions. That's the way Thomas read them at the time and still does read them. Back then Jesus simply had things to say and needed to size up the situation, for some day in the near future he would be taking Jerusalem by storm. And, when that day arrived, he would simply go ahead and do it.

Their sojourn into Tyre and Sidon, Thomas is convinced, has everything to do with those pagan outposts themselves and nothing to do with what happened in Sychar or in Herod's dungeon. In what ways will their Gentile neighbors be brought into the compass of Jesus' kingdom of heaven? That and the nature of that kingdom are what preoccupy his thoughts.

Levi Matthew apparently wonders much the same things. "Do the man's designs extend to this ancient land beside the Great Sea?" he asks Thomas along the way. "For hundreds of years our fathers fought these people. Will our sons be doing the same?"

"My first reaction is no. It doesn't fit him," Thomas responds.

"Nor do I think so either. The boundaries of his kingdom might not be as territorial as we at first assumed, and its tenants might be defined by something other than bloodlines. It's all so vague right now, but I'm reluctant to rule out anything. His kingdom is beginning to become as enigmatic as the man himself. Be surprised at nothing."

"Could what you just said be tangential to his born again declaration?" Thomas asks. "That one continues to haunt me. Keeps me awake at night."

"Tell me about it."

"You too?"

Matthew nods his head. "Has to be a metaphor. But for what? That a man must be born again was what he told the young Pharisee down in Jerusalem. Nicodemus. To my recollection he's never used the figure around us before or since. Just that one time when he was telling us about their meeting. If it was of such vital importance, why would he not say it to us or to some of his crowds? The Pharisees are lining up against him. Why one of them and not us?"

"We only have that one snippet from his conversation with Nicodemus that night, and they must have talked a lot. He was gone quite awhile. We don't know the context. We don't know whether he just volunteered it out of the blue or if it was part of his answer to something Nicodemus might have asked him."

"He's full of surprises, but to keep something as crucial as that from us seems awfully strange, don't you think?"

"Could it be more than a metaphor, Levi?" Thomas wants to know.

"How so?"

"I'm not suggesting he meant it literally, just that actual physical birth might possibly have been apart of the equation—that is, if it were somehow germane to what the Pharisee wanted to know. You hear what I'm saying?"

"You lost me when you gave up a perfectly good metaphor. Not like you, friend."

"Think about it, Levi. People of this fellow's station have asked honest questions of him when we were around. Most of the time to accuse him or trick him—that I grant you—but occasionally simply because they wanted to know what he had to say. They were sincere. This Pharisee wanted a quiet personal conversation with him. Just the two of them. What are the two question that, in one form or another, they always get around to asking him?"

"First they want to know if he is indeed the Christ."

"Exactly! And, if he doesn't deny it, the next thing they want to know is how they can pass through the gates into his kingdom. Is that not what you've observed too?"

"Definitely yes, every time I'd say."

"That is also my observation. They want to know what gets them into the camp. Especially after they've heard all the rumors about his opening the door to publicans and sinners, cutthroats, Samaritans, and possibly even a Roman or two—all the time when in their own minds they're the leading candidates. You can almost see the wheels turning."

"They assume they're already in."

"Right. By token of being the heirs of Abraham, Isaac, and Jacob, they simply assume they're automatically in any kingdom of the righteous that comes along. They want Jesus to confirm that status."

"Yes, I think you're right."

"And so he maybe told this Pharisee that automatic inclusion is no longer going to be the case."

"A very live possibility. Think. Maybe he was effectively saying, 'Not so fast, my man. Being of the seed of Abraham is no longer the key to the kingdom. Bloodline's no longer going to get you there.

The chosen to my kingdom will be defined by something other than birth.' Faith would be my personal guess."

"A spiritual birth of some sort certainly. Yes, faith fits."

"Faith not family."

"Belief rather than birth from now on. Anyway, that's the conclusion I've come to at this point. Maybe I'll think better of it tomorrow."

"Could be a stretch, but you might be onto something."

"Anyway it's a riddle I think he wants us at least to keep trying to figure out."

"Your take does fit the context both of Nicodemus' question and of Jesus' opening the door to Samaritans and his treatment of some out-and-out Gentiles. If that's the case, it might also redefine the nature and constituency of his kingdom as well."

"And, as we agree, it does bring faith into the picture front and center. He's big on faith."

"Huge."

After they cross over into Phoenicia, they head toward the coast to intercept the roadway that takes them toward the major cities. In every village they pass through, blatantly pagan all, they find individuals who have heard of Jesus. He's already as much the celebrity in neighboring communities as in any of the towns of Israel. Men ripe in years, women holding infants, and scores upon scores of children line the roadways to catch glimpses of the Master as he comes into view. They call out his name.

In one of the towns north of Tyre just south of Sidon, a woman, Greek in her features and tongue, breaks from the other onlookers to fall at Jesus' feet. She looks up into his face and in her own language cries out, "Come, heal my daughter! She has convulsions and seizures. I fear devils are loose inside of her."

Although his eyes are full of pity, Jesus proceeds on his way.

"She stiffens and writhes and has the strength of ten," the woman persists, following him, continuing to plead. "Her teeth grind and froth issues from her lips. It's getting worse all the time. You're a miracle-worker, they say, who comes from God. You can heal her. I know you can. Good sir, please come!"

Jesus stops.

Judas Iscariot, immediately behind him, tugs at his cloak. "Best to send her on her way," he says. "She's creating a scene, making a spectacle of herself and us as well. Best we be about our business."

Looking down at the distraught mother, Jesus says, almost apologetically, "My mission, dear woman, is to the needy children of Israel. That you must know."

Slumped prostrate at Jesus' feet and, reaching out with her fingers to touch the fringes of his garment, she pleads, "Do help me, please! Oh, good sir, please help!"

"You know the children of the family must first have their fill," he says next, emotion in his face. "One can't just take their food and toss it to the household pets. That simply is not done."

"Yes, I know that, I know that," the frantic mother replies, "but even the household pets get a chance now and then to lick up the scraps that fall from the children's plates."

This response clearly delights Jesus. A broad smile stretches over his face. "Well said, my dear woman, very well said," he tells her, "and true. Others suffer from lack of faith, but not you. Certainly not you. It's okay for you to go home now. Your little girl is healed. Go see for yourself."

With that, he and his disciples continue on their way.

And the Gentile woman, gathering herself up from the grime of the roadway, the disciples soon learn, then goes promptly home to discover, yes, it is so. Her little daughter is indeed healed.

"Exactly what we were talking about on our way up," says Thomas later to Matthew, as they continue to move north.

"And not a speck of ambiguity about this one," replies the older man, "purebred Gentile, one hundred percent, no cross. She was not about to let go, pressed her point all the way. Begged his mercy and got it. She believed him, believed in him—whatever—and he healed her little girl. I've never seen him smile more broadly."

"Her ancestors, you realize, were King David's bitterest enemies.

Makes you wonder just where the boundaries of his kingdom are going to reach," muses Thomas.

"I notice we're still headed north."

Before Thomas can respond to Matthew's observation, they find Judas Iscariot wedging his way between them. It is immediately apparent that he does not share their elation. "What was that scene all about?" he growls, looking first to the one and then to the other.

"Faith," Matthew is quick to reply. "My guess is faith. It's a huge thing with him right now. 'Oh, you of little faith!' he's said in one context or another a dozen times if he's said it once. What I think he most wants is for people to believe him and in him. Believe, believe, and believe, he's always telling us. By her faith that woman is now one of us."

"Which, if you're right, means being of Abraham's seed doesn't even matter?" Iscariot snaps back. "Is that what you're saying?"

"It is entirely possible that Abraham's seed is now more faith than it is family."

"So she, and by inference everybody like her, is now in the camp of the chosen!" says the Judean, aghast. "He's to be the Savior of Israel. Isn't that the prophecy? King of the Jews. Have we not been told that since we were children? I don't understand. First he opened the gate to the publican, then the Roman slave, and then the Samaritans and now to the Gentiles. He once said the gate was narrow. Now it seems wide open to anyone and everyone who wants to come in. I don't understand. Who's left for him to save us from? The Pharisees? The theologians? Our own spiritual hierarchy? Who?"

"It's his kingdom, isn't it?" says Thomas. "Who knows who's going to be in it? Seems as though he can have anybody he chooses".

"It flies in the face of everything, all our expectations," Iscariot continues to bemoan. "David's kingdom was one of tight organization. Samuel and Abner stood behind him. A great army was at his beck and call. His subjects were merchants and tradesmen, priests, teachers, shopkeepers, shepherds, farmers, and workmen—all of his own lineage."

"This is a greater than David," Thomas tells him. "Might we then be on the lookout for a more expansive kingdom than his?"

"Others not of our blood were in David's kingdom too but were treated as strangers within his gates. They weren't in the legitimate mix."

"In this new kingdom apparently some of them are going to be."

"Which means we're running out of people to be saved from."

"Which means we might have to redefine *saved*. Doesn't it?"

"Something's askew, terribly askew! Don't you see it?"

With that Judas Iscariot retreats further back in their train to restate his case to Simon the Zealot but, from what Thomas can see, gets no consolation from him either and so elects to walk alone, trailing all the others. Back there by himself, he gesticulates and mumbles—no outbreaks for the others to hear, just mumbles, like a troubled child whose pipedreams have suddenly crumbled all around him. His ever growing distance from the other disciples underscores his disillusionment.

The Zealot and Judas early on seemed to be on the same wave length, but no longer. Simon, anticipating that soon or late a great mass movement will sweep Jesus to his throne, seems content to wait. He does not fall back, as he'd previously done, to be with his old friend Iscariot. Nor does Thomas, his new friend, help him to reason matters through either, this mostly because he is himself at a loss to give explanation to Jesus' words and ways. He also sometimes fantasizes the hordes descending upon the Holy City to lift the Master to his throne, but quickly cautions himself that there is no guarantee that that will happen. Jesus has so far said nothing specifically. The Christ will come into his kingdom, but the when, where and how are increasingly fuzzy. The Twin has nothing of comfort to offer his fellow disciples at all.

"He is to be the savoir of Israel, is he not?" Thomas asks Matthew on their way back south a week or so later. "That is one of the designations in the prophecies about him?"

"It is."

"Who then exactly is he to save Israel from? That's what's got friend Judas in a tizzy. Apparently Jesus is good with the Romans and good with the Samaritans. And now it looks as though he's good with Goliath's progeny too. He's opening the gates to everybody. Iscariot's worried sick that there isn't going to be anybody left for him to save us from. I do have a more than mild curiosity myself."

"And, being in that fringe element myself, I'm wondering as well," Matthew tells him.

"So what precisely does 'being saved' mean?"

"Well, I'd say it usually means people being snatched from danger or threats or maybe from other people who are out there to get them or bad people who already have. That's how you'd generally hear it used."

"When the prophets spoke of the savior of Israel, was it not in that sense?" asks Thomas.

Matthew pauses before answering. "It would seem so," he then says.

"In more or less a political sense then, would you think?"

"Although it could be that Jesus has his own twist to it. He often does, you know."

"What kind of a twist?"

"That whatever we're to be saved from has ceased to be political altogether, that maybe the whole issue has nothing to do with Romans, Macedonians, Persians, Babylonians, Assyrians, or Philistines, that it's a little more abstract than battlements and battalions."

"Such as?" Thomas wants to know.

"Our own worse selves, our own darker sides. The evil that lurks in the hearts of men. You must have felt it yourself sometime: What you want to do, indeed know you should do, you don't do, and what you don't want to do, that's exactly what you wind up doing. You're prisoner to your own nature! It's like you're chained to a deadweight and can't shake it off. However hard you try, you cannot break free! You think you're free, but you're not! No more than a galley slave! Forgive me, Thomas. I'm just thinking out loud—universalizing again on my own little war within."

"What you speak of may turn out to be more universal than you expect. A thought occurred to me just now as well. Is it possible, do you think, that we're looking at all of this upside down? That maybe Jesus is more out to save us for some thing than from somebody? I'm given to thinking out loud too."

"I would not dismiss that possibility at all."

Some weeks after this, when they return to Capernaum and Jesus is questioned by a theologian, the Twin has occasion to recall his whole dialogue with Matthew. The question in this instance, he realizes at once, is probably little more than a ploy to discredit Jesus in the eyes of the people. Most questions from Pharisees and theologians lately have been that.

"Master," the theologian, overly politely, asks, "what must I do to guarantee eternal life?"

"You're an expert in the Law," Jesus answers him. "What conclusions have you come to as a result all of your studies?"

"The Law says we must love God with all our hearts, souls, strength and minds," the theological scholar replies, "and our neighbors as ourselves."

"Excellent," Jesus says. "Go ahead and do just that, and eternal life will be yours."

"But, Master, exactly who is my neighbor?"

"I have a little story that might clarify that," Jesus tells him. "There was once a man on his way from Jerusalem to Jericho who was set upon by a gang of robbers. They stole his money and goods and ripped off his clothes and bludgeoned him so severely that he was almost dead, then went on their way. Well, before long a priest happened to be traveling that same road and saw him there. What did he do? He walked right on past him, never breaking his stride. Later a Levite came upon the scene. What he did was to cross the road before passing him. He didn't want to get too close, you understand.

"Then, a little while after this, along came a Samaritan traveler. When he saw the robbers' victim lying there, bloodied and gasping for life, he was moved with compassion for him and hastened over to him and nursed his wounds with oil and wine and then bandaged him up and hoisted him onto his own pack animal. He took him to an inn where he continued to attend his injuries. The next morning he paid the innkeeper for both their keeps out of his own pocket and then gave him two extra denarii. 'Attend to him well, will you,' he said, 'and I'll take care of any additional expense on my return trip.'

"Now I ask you," Jesus then says, "which of these three treated this brutally beaten man like a neighbor?"

"The man who accorded him practical sympathy," the theologian answers.

"Good. That's right," Jesus says. "So why don't you go out and do the same?"

"Boy, he just loves those Samaritans, doesn't he?" Iscariot cannot help saying in Thomas's hearing as Jesus' interrogator and his companion slink away

"He seems to love everybody that's had a bad shake," Thomas responds. "Remember on the mountain that one day what he said about the poverty-stricken? Said that someday they'd inherit the earth. Maybe he's going to see to it that they do."

"His favorite down-and-outers are somehow always Samaritans and their ilk though. Ever notice?"

Mary the Magdalene

DEMON POSSESSION IS something Thomas cannot get his mind around. It is a convenient term and has become an easy label for aberrations of mind and body that defy ready explanation. He has searched the Laws and the Histories and the Prophets for ancient reports of it and has come up dry. Not even a word about it in the Scriptures so far as he can tell, much less any clue as to how the notion originated. He wonders if maybe it's a Babylonian thing or a Persian thing brought back to Israel by returning exiles. The Persians were especially famous for being into demons and such.

And so it is that he brings up the topic with Scripture-expert Levi Matthew, who knows of no mention of it in the Scriptures either. "But it's a useful term," he insists, "Like 'rats in the attic,' people know what it means. Say someone's 'demon-possessed,' and everybody has a picture of what's going on."

"Yes," Thomas agrees, "but the language suggests a cause that isn't the real cause at all. It conjures up a picture of little bitty evil aliens wreaking havoc somewhere under a person's skin, when in reality there's an impaired mind disorder. Maybe the guy who's 'demon-possessed' was dropped on his head when he was a baby. Who knows?"

"Still a useful tag. The number of demons people assign a person indicates the severity and frequency of his seizures. Jesus doesn't seem critical of it."

"We don't know that he buys it or just goes along with it," says Thomas. "He does heal the demon-possessed, I'll give you that much. Nobody else has any luck with it at all."

Thomas is reminded of this conversation some time later when they are traveling through Magdala, a port town across Gennesaret from Capernaum. They slip into the agora virtually unnoticed, a rarity these days. There is a crowd there, a considerable one. People are standing in a semicircle not far away but not to greet them, as has sometimes been the case. Patently oblivious to their celebrated guests, they are totally preoccupied with something else that's going on.

As Jesus and company approach, through the gaps in the crowd they can see a young woman shaking violently, then freezing in place and suddenly slumping to the ground. The crowd is keeping a safe distance from her, as if watching a house afire or curs going for each other's throats, while she continues to writhe and then suddenly becomes rigid in the dust of the street.

"Her devils got her again," an older woman says as she backs further away.

"Seven of them! Imagine. No help for her," says another, "not with seven. She'll be swallowing her tongue one of these days. Happens, you know."

The crowd merely looks on, concern in some of their faces and unveiled excitement in those of others. Some lean in to see her better but quickly withdraw. One man reaches out to touch her on the leg. When the leg suddenly jerks stiff, the man jolts off balance backward into the fellow behind him. This amuses several of the men. Under their breath they make crude comments to each other and snicker.

It is then that Jesus breaks through their ranks and crouches down beside the woman, who by now is absolutely still. He puts his arm under her shoulders to lift her, at the same time speaking to her softly. The crowd gawks at him, some recognizing him, a few simply curious as to who he is and what he's doing. After some time the young woman comes to. She opens her eyes and looks about, finally fastening them on Jesus, as he helps her to her feet. The people seem amazed.

"Never came out of it that fast before," says the women who first spoke earlier.

"Never so lively when she did. Will you look at her! Like she's just woken up from a nap," observes the other.

The crowd opens up as Jesus, his arm still about the stricken woman's shoulders, guides her to a grassy spot in the shade of a building where she can sit down. Some on-lookers quickly withdraw from the scene to go back to their respective places of business to haggle and sell. Others, women primarily, stay on to encircle Jesus and the demoniac he has just healed. His disciples stand back to make room for them. The women pick up their conversation.

"Not even trembling. How's that for you?"

"Usually limp like a sodden shank of wool. Not this time. Not even gasping for breath. Sitting up there's cool's can be."

"Smiling now. Will you look at that!"

"Not something the cat left on the doorstep anymore. Relaxed, strong, as normal as you please."

"Never thought I'd see the likes of this."

Thomas and Levi Matthew, who have witnessed such scenes before, listen to them talk. Neither man says anything. Much of their joy in being with Jesus is moments like this, when profound compassion and unearthly power intersect. It has the stamp of God himself upon it. They too are in awe.

"You're right," says Thomas, as they prepare to travel, "the label really doesn't matter. Call it what you may, the healing anyway is supernatural."

"I would say so," replies Matthew. "And, like most that you and I have seen of late, an act of compassion. He genuinely loves the unloved and unlovely. Curious, wouldn't you say? Seem to be his people."

"I agree," comes in Judas Iscariot, near them, "but not a firm foundation for a kingdom, I wouldn't think."

"He's the only foundation his kingdom will ever need," says Thomas.

"What we've witnessed here," Matthew breaks in, "may speak more to the scope of his kingdom than its hierarchy. It's definitely not the realm we always imagined. On that I agree"

"His kingdom's as much a riddle as the man himself."

It is a surprise to no one that, when they leave Magdala, the young woman comes with them. Her name, like Jesus' own mother's, is Mary. She joins the small corps of women already in Jesus' entourage: the other Mary; Joanna, the wife of Herod's steward; and Susanna. These have been drawing from their own resources to provide Jesus and his disciples with food and clean clothes and such things as they have need of. The Magdalene, having nothing, brings only herself.

Thomas gets to know her.

"Many has he healed," he tells her some time later on the road. "Most return in health to their families and friends, to what they were doing before, to new lives in old places. You have joined his train. I'm curious to know why."

"The only life I have is the life I have in him," she tells him.

"What of your parents?"

"They're gone. Little enough was the joy I ever brought them. For the better part of their lives I was a millstone about their poor necks. On my best days I was a fragile, pitiful being and on my worst a disreputable spectacle convulsing in the street, object for the sport and amusement of unfeeling rogues. I wished for death, but death would not take me. Great is the burden that has been lifted from me. I am no longer that woman. I feel . . .."

"Born anew?"

"Yes, that. I love him, not as a woman loves a man but as she loves her savior. You men each gave up something to follow him. The brothers Bar-Jonah and brothers Bar Zebedee their fishing nets, Matthew his tax booth, others their homes. I don't know about you, Thomas. I gave up seven devils and a life of madness."

Thomas does not think to ask her what she means by this.

Within the month they are invited to the home of a Pharisee. It's an invitation that Judas Iscariot, give him credit, strongly urges Jesus not to accept. "They consider you their enemy, an insurgent maybe, a heretic certainly," he says. "They mean you no good."

Jesus recalls for the Judean's sake that Nicodemus, the young

Pharisee he conferred with in Jerusalem, merely wanted to ask him some questions and turned out to be a rather pleasant fellow. He sees no reason not to expect the same of this one.

"Do you not know they meet almost daily now to entrap you, do everything in their power to bring you down by fair means and foul?"

Jesus assures him again there's nothing to worry about and invites those in his entourage who would like to join him to do so. Most of his disciples so choose, as also does Mary the Magdalene. They arrive respectably early for a meal that is respectably late but are comfortably seated in the foyer to bide their time.

Another woman, not of their ranks, has trailed the invited guests into the house but does not take a seat. Shabbily attired and ill groomed, she brings something of the street into the room with her. They pretend not to notice her until, all of a sudden, she drops to her knees directly in front of Jesus and begins to swab his feet with scented oil. Her face lights up in a rhapsodic glow as tears form in either eye and she begins to weep pronouncedly but softly as she goes about her task. Her tears mix with the ointment as she works it in, weeping profusely all the while. Her face almost to the floor, she wipes his feet with her hair, holding each in turn adoringly, affectionately as one might hold and fondle a rare gem or a delicate piece of pottery, kissing them repeatedly as she weeps afresh. Jesus lets this happen.

Thomas is touched by what he is witnessing.

"Now if you were a true prophet," the host, loudly clearing his throat, finally says to Jesus, "you would have known what kind of woman this is. Oh yes, you would have known she's . . . a harlot."

"Listen to me," replies Jesus. "There was a man once who had two debtors. One owed him five hundred denarii and the other only fifty. When neither could pay he forgave both debts. Now which of these two debtors would you say loved him more?"

"Well," answers the Pharisee, "probably the one with the greater debt."

"Exactly," says Jesus. "Now don't you see what's happened here?

When I came into your house you felt no need to wash my feet, nor were you moved to anoint my head with oil. This woman has bathed my feet with her own tears. She has kissed them unceasingly and wiped them with her hair and rubbed them with ointment. Yes, her sins are many, and therefore much has she been forgiven."

All the while he speaks, the woman continues to kiss his feet and weep.

"A setup," whispers Iscariot, immediately to the right of Thomas.

"Very likely," Thomas agrees.

Mary the Magdalene, to Thomas's left, watching on in stone silence, does not peep until they have finished their visit and are all back on the road together. She has been moved as no one else in their company has been. That much is obvious.

"They've postured themselves as his enemies," Thomas tries to explain to her. "Will do anything to expose him, in the process of which they expose only themselves."

"She was genuine," the Magdalene tells him.

"Seemed every bit so."

"My heart went out to her. I identified with her. If she were suddenly taken in hand and forced from the room, I would have rushed in to kneel in her place and pick up where she left off. Were she my own sister, I could not have felt closer to her than I did back there."

"I hear you."

"How can people be so cruel? That's something I've never been able to understand."

"It's something you're going to have to expect from these people, the Pharisees and theologians I mean. They have a sick need to be right and to be righteous—to appear that way to others anyway. God is on their side, so they can do anything through anybody at anytime they want. They see themselves as having a holy mandate."

"Knew something was up, but didn't quite expect that," Iscariot, at Thomas's' left, comes in.

"Yes," says Thomas, "they seem to have switched strategies. He's too much to take on anymore in the streets or the synagogues."

"His answers are either too cryptic for them to follow, making them look tongue-tied, or too pointed, so they wind up skewered on the spits of their own questions. Therefore they feign civility while doing their best to lay snares for him."

"If it weren't so ruthless and pathetic, it'd be comical."

Miracles of a Different Kind

"**Y**OU HAVE TO give it to him, pitying the pitiful the way he does," Judas Iscariot says to Thomas en route back to Capernaum, "but he isn't building much of a base in the process, I'd have to say. Patches them up and they go their ways. Not one in ten falls in behind him. The Magdalene is the exception, not the rule."

"But for every one he heals his reputation improves tenfold," replies Thomas. "That should fit your schemata for the masses descending on Jerusalem."

"It makes people sit up and take notice, to be sure, but does nothing to sway the kind of people he'll eventually need. He needs men of station, not a ragtag mob of the possessed and dispossessed, men people know and admire. Like that young Pharisee down in Jerusalem he befuddled with riddles and metaphors. Put men the likes of him at his side and you've got something to build on."

"You mean instead of men like you and me?"

"The two don't have to be mutually exclusive. A great kingdom needs its subordinates as well as its regents, its providers as well as its foot soldiers and, not least, a treasury that will require far more than a single shallow purse."

"Nothing he's so far said," Thomas tells the Judean, "so much as suggests that, territorially or organizationally, his kingdom and the one you envision are one and the same."

"It will," Iscariot assures him. "The new David's kingdom will not lack the luster of the first's. It will be far, far more grand."

"To that I agree. But the question is: In what ways will it be more grand?"

The two disciples continue to converse ardently in this vein, neither one noticing where they are or what is going on about them or the fact that Jesus has suddenly been accosted by a man of no small standing in the city—instantly recognized by both of them, when they do glance about, as a chief officer of the synagogue nearby. His name they do not have to be told: Jairus. Few people of the city enjoy the repute and admiration of this leader. Judas Iscariot's lips in a flash break into broad smile upon seeing him rush toward Jesus and throw himself at the Master's feet.

"My little girl is dying!" he cries out. "Come, I pray, and lay your hands upon her that she might be healed and live!"

Saying nothing, Jesus motions for Jairus to lead the way.

Their trek to the synagogue dignitary's home is briefly interrupted by a woman along the street—as dowdy and undistinguished as Jairus, leading Jesus, is the opposite—who also seeks Jesus' healing power. When Jesus stops to oblige her, Thomas can see his fellow disciple's face quickly transformed from one almost euphoric to one bespeaking impatience bordering on disgust. Soon on their way, Judas briefly brightens up again.

Before they reach their destination, however, someone from Jairus's house meets them. Tears fill the man's eyes. "You need not bother the master," he tells the heavy-hearted father. "Your daughter is dead."

Poor Jairus, unable to comprehend what is just told him, trembles, and then tears burst from his already reddened eyes as he turns to Jesus to thank him anyway. Tenderly, reassuringly Jesus speaks first.

"Do not be afraid," he says, "but believe."

Then, motioning for Peter, James, and John quickly to his side, he proceeds to Jairus's estate, where, John later tells Thomas, they find people are standing about the porch and anteroom moaning and sobbing unashamedly. When they see Jairus, they fall on his shoulders and weep louder than ever.

"Why do you make such a racket with your crying?" Jesus asks them. "The little girl is not dead. She's only asleep."

Those who apparently saw her die scoff at him, but they do go outside when he asks them to. He then bids his three disciples and the child's parents go with him into the room where their little daughter is lying motionless on her bed. It is plain to see why the people scoffed. The pallid cast of death is already on the girl's features; there is no sign of breath or life within her.

Jesus reaches down and takes her limp, pale hand. "Wake up, little girl," he says. "You've slept long enough. It's now time to wake up."

Her eyes suddenly blink open, and in an instant her cheeks and slender arms blush with life. A smile breaks from her lips, and, as if no more than awakening after a long and restful sleep, she bounds from her bed and skips about the room. Jairus and his wife cannot contain their joy, and it is clear that Jesus heartily shares in it with them. He asks them not to say anything to anyone about it, then suggests they prepare their little daughter a normal breakfast. And after that he and his company leave.

As they withdraw from Jairus's house, Thomas remarks to John, "His power seems to extend even over death itself. Or was it that the child, as he said, was only sleeping after all?"

"She looked dead."

"But he said she was only sleeping, like that woman's son at Nain. You think that maybe to him death and sleep might possibly be the same thing?"

"You mean could it be another instance of what you said the Greeks have a name for? I don't know. What I can tell you is that he sincerely felt her parents' heartbreak as though it were his own. You could see it in his eyes. And he felt their jubilation when she stirred to life again."

"But everybody there, you say, is convinced he resurrected her from the dead?"

John nods vigorously. "Including her parents—especially them."

"Tomorrow, despite his instructions to the contrary, they'll be telling the world."

Thomas turns out to be almost on target in his prediction. Jairus and his wife do tell the world all right, but do so right away, that very day, rather than wait for the morrow. With all their close friends and an equal number of strangers, as soon as their daughter finishes her wakeup meal, they go about their immediate neighborhood telling the story of how Jesus raised their daughter from the dead.

This puts the synagogue leader at odds with some of the local Pharisees, but a father's delight over Jesus' bringing his little daughter out of death's shadows trumps any allegiance he has to the spiritual hierarchy of the city. Jairus does not theorize about Jesus' calling or his role in their collective future. The man intervened to save his child, and at the moment that is all that matters.

"Call it a miracle, call it magic, call it happy coincidence. Whatever you will. I call it a breakthrough. He's lining up the pillars," is Iscariot's take on the incident.

"One pillar does not a temple make," Thomas tells him.

"Which is exactly why we must have more."

Before their brief excursion into Judea, Thomas and Judas Iscariot do agree on one thing: namely, that it is nigh unto impossible for the crowds Jesus is drawing to get any larger. As time goes on, however, both jubilant, they marvel at how utterly wrong their assumption has turned out to be. The healing at Magdala has resulted in more followers up and down the western shore of Gennesaret, but that of Jairus's daughter has brought out even more from the ranks of the synagogue elite. Men and women hitherto cowed by the Pharisees and theologians swell the throngs that fall in behind the celebrated Nazarene.

Well over a year has passed since the Master first appeared on the scene, and in every town, every district he and his train now enter, great hordes of people gather, thicker than sheep at the feeding racks or bees around the honeycombs. The crowds are ever upon them now, more people than a body can count. There is no town in Galilee Jesus can go anymore without women walking away from their looms and ovens, men their oxcarts and sheaves, children their play to catch glimpses of the famed miracle-worker, perhaps to touch his robe or, if infirm, to have him speak the words that will deliver them whole. His is a name now on everyone's lips.

Because of the great crowds pressing upon their company from all sides, Jesus one day retreats into a deserted area where not so much as a hut can be seen for leagues in any direction. But still the multitudes continue to descend from every direction. Hundreds come out to see him, and as the day goes on they number into the thousands; by late afternoon, Thomas and Matthew estimate, maybe as many as five thousand.

Jesus mingles among them and then stands slightly apart to speak of the things months earlier he told his disciples one day on the mountain. He tells stories of farmers planting their fields and women ecstatic over finding lost pearls and shepherds searching for missing lambs. He speaks without apparent effort, his voice moderate and mellow but with sufficient volume to reach the ears at the farthest fringes of his audience. At moments he has them smiling, once in a while laughing outrightly, and then brings a somber hush over them with the effect that they experience a profound awe, wondering if perhaps they are standing on holy ground.

It is late afternoon when he finishes.

Thomas, standing next to Mary the Magdalene, sees Jesus' facial muscles suddenly go slack. "Something's troubling him," he tells her.

Turning to Andrew, closest of the disciples to him right then, Jesus says, "There are so many of them, and they have been here so much of the day."

"Should we send them away?" Iscariot asks him.

Jesus shakes his head. "They have to be very, very hungry by this time," he says in response. "We should feed them before they go. It'll be a long time before many of them can get home. Some might not make it."

"You'd think they were all his own children," whispers the Magdalene to Thomas.

"Where are we going to find food to feed them all?" Judas wants to know.

The women in the company glance quickly at one another, each holding out her hands, empty palms up. Quickly the disciples scurry about amidst the multitude. It is Andrew who discovers what might be the only edibles in the crowd, which is a satchel of food a boy happens to have along for his own meal: five small barley loaves and two smoked fish.

Andrew brings the boy forward and has him show the bread and fish to Jesus. "Not much for a crowd like this," he says apologetically.

"Have the people sit down on the grass," Jesus tells them.

Then he raises his voice to the heavens to bless the food and sends his disciples out into the crowd to distribute it as far as it will go. It seems that the first three or four men grab up everything there is; but as they pass the basket along, others take from it as well and begin to eat. The disciples blink their eyes in amazement. As much as the people take, the basket is always full.

Everyone there eats his fill, and there are far, far more scraps left over than the original fish and bread they started with. Jesus' face beams with obvious delight as he watches the people rise up refreshed. Thomas, still at the Magdalene's side, finds himself also smiling as he has never in his life smiled before.

"Strive not for bread that does not last, but rather for bread that's eternal," Jesus tells his close followers after the crowd disperses. "He who gives that to you bears the stamp of his father."

"A feat the likes of which we have not seen so far," says Levi Matthew to Thomas en route back to Capernaum. "Nowhere in all the Scriptures—not in the Laws, not in the Prophets, not in the Histories—do we find a man who can do the things this one does. There is not one thing he cannot do."

"The Pharisees and theologians'll have some explanation by the end of the week," Thomas tells him.

"True, they won't let it go. They'll think of something."

They are right. The disciples are not back in Capernaum for three days before their ears are picking up the skeptics' version of what happened out in nowhere land. What is agreed upon by most of the Pharisees and theologians is that there was indeed a multitude that followed Jesus and his company into the wilds somewhere, though there could not have been more than five or six hundred of them, and, yes, they had plenty of food to go around when they got hungry. But what really happened was that, like anybody in his right mind, each had brought along something to eat. Who, after all, strays that far from home without a morsel or two tucked away under his robe or in a satchel? When some youngster pulled out his stash to nibble a bit, so did everyone else. They passed the goodies around and had a good old fashioned picnic for themselves. That was all. Just a matter of sharing. It's really heartening that he teaches them to share. But no miracle is that! Pshaw!

The other people around Capernaum, however, seem to prefer the version some of them personally witnessed and participated in themselves. It is only later that it dawns upon most of them that they'd participated in an honest to goodness miracle.

Huge crowds, although glorious spectacles to the kingdom-dreamers in Jesus' retinue, did turn out occasionally to be problematic to the Master himself. Seldom lately has he been able to gather his disciples together for private instruction. And, with the prospect of sending them out on their own in the immediate future, this has become a matter of no small concern.

Early one morning, weeks now after his feeding the multitude, down on the shores of Gennesaret he proceeds to discuss with his men what they are to do and say when they go out to represent him in the various areas he will be sending them; he is soon, however, interrupted by people crowding in behind them. He tries to include them as well in what he says. Throughout the rest of the morning and on into the afternoon more and more people amass around him. Some want to be healed of one thing or another. He obliges them but soon gets back to addressing the growing throng. There is no letup.

Finally, with a gesture of his hand toward a boat half in the water and half out, he says, "Let's go to the other side."

And so his men all climb into the boat and push off. It is strange, they reflect later looking back on it, that no one breathes a word about the weather. Peter or James usually studies the skies and checks the direction of the wind before they sail, but this time no one so much as glances at the clouds or lifts a finger to the wind. It might have been because of the wearisome tasks of the day or because of the pressing crowd; but, whatever the reason, no one thinks to mention the weather.

And someone should have.

They are nearly halfway across when the winds begin to pick up. There are black clouds above them. Most of the crew think little of it until they can see fixed ridges of fear in Peter's face, then Andrew's and John's. And suddenly the squall is upon them.

Thomas looks back toward the stern where Jesus, shortly after their casting off, has plopped himself across some nets and has immediately fallen asleep. He is still sleeping, and the calm beauty of his face strikes the disciple. It clashes with the violent storm that rages about them; it clashes with the hard world of reality he himself has come to know. For a fleeting instant Jesus, to Thomas anyway, seems detached from the world he lives in, as though actually not a part of it.

The men quickly hand around the pails. Already the ever-mounting waves have covered the bottom of the boat with ankle-deep water. Each dip brings the level higher. Many, many times Thomas has been on the sea, but never in a storm of such violence and fury. The look on Peter's face and John's tell him neither have they. They all work frantically bailing the water out with all their strength. It is now about their knees.

Jesus is still at the stern and still asleep.

Judas Iscariot, with the tacit consent of all, suddenly rushes toward him and screams, "Master! Master, we're perishing! Don't you care?"

It's strange but typical, reflects Thomas later. Half their number have all but been born on the sea. The sea was their home, their life; the sea was their work and play. Until just short of two years ago the sea was all they really knew. Yet in this desperate moment they turn in unison not to Peter or James, not to John or Andrew, but to Jesus.

Once more Iscariot shouts, "Master! We're perishing!" this time shaking Jesus at the shoulder.

Jesus slowly stands to his feet and reaches for a rope to steady himself as the boat drops to the hollow of another wave. With his free hand he wipes the spray from his face and looks at his followers.

His eyes fall on them one at a time. Then turning, he lifts up his arms as might an imperial prince answering the cheers of a crowd; and in gentle tones that can mysteriously be heard above the din of the turbulent sea he says, "Peace. Be still."

Immediately the towering waves about them collapse, and the tumultuous storm becomes a quiet, motionless calm. His disciples are calm too, momentarily, as he once more looks at them and, slowly shaking his head, says with great disappointment in his voice, "Oh, you of little faith!"

Gradually a new sensation of fear comes over Thomas—no longer the fear of being swallowed up by churning waters but a more subtle fear, not a fear of the natural but a fear of the preternatural. The powers of Jesus in healings and miracles have by now become commonplace, but the proportions of this act leave him aghast.

"What manner of man is he anyway?" he asks.

The same question is asked up and down the coast, for this incident too is blazed across the land. So there is not a soul now in all of Galilee who does not know who Jesus is.

Even the Tetrarch Herod within days of the feat knows about it and has reasons of his own to be greatly perturbed. This the disciples learn through Joanna's husband, Herod's personal steward. Prior to this time the Roman puppet has been humored and only mildly curious about tales of lepers being cleansed, blind men being given their sight, deaf people their hearing, withered hands restored, and devils driven from the demon-possessed.

But, when told that the man from Nazareth called out for the winds to cease and the waves to become calm and that Nature immediately acquiesced, the simpleton governor becomes frightened indeed.

"It's John the Baptizer back from the dead!" he cries. "His ghost is behind this! I know that's it!"

Herod then doubles his personal guard, Joanna's husband tells his wife and she her fellows in Jesus' train. "He's cowering in the innermost chambers of his fortress, muttering nonsense about avenging ghosts," she reports.

When word of this reaches Jesus, he evidences neither amusement nor fear, nor does he inquire into the details. "What does interest me," he tells his disciples, "is what others, the people, in general, think. What are they saying?"

"Rumors are all over the place," Peter tells him. "Some, like Herod, think you're the Baptizer back from the grave. Others Jeremiah. Still others that you're maybe Elijah or some other prophet out of the past."

"And you? What exactly are your perceptions? If someone were to ask you, say, who or what I'm like, whom you would compare me to? What would you tell him?"

"A messenger from on high dispatched by God Himself," Peter answers right away.

"And you, dear Matthew?" Jesus asks the onetime tax collector.

"A thinker of the first order, I'd tell him," says Levi Matthew after some thought. "The greatest ever, greater than all the Greeks put together, greater than the Prophets, greater than Moses himself."

"And you, dear Thomas. Whom would you compare me to?"

Thomas ponders this. "Nobody," he finally answers. "You are like no one or nothing I've ever known. To me, I must confess, you are an utter mystery."

Preparations

J UDAS ISCARIOT IS still trying to enlist Thomas in his none-too-subtle efforts of late to reconcile Jesus and the Pharisees and, when he fails to do so, he immediately looks to his once close friend Simon the Zealot. And, when the Zealot turns deaf ear, he's back to courting Thomas. "You're a thinker," the Judean says, "not like these sheep. Got a mind of your own and a good ear for hearing what's really said, not what you want to hear."

"And, for all that, I hardly know a thing," Thomas tells him.

"He's alienating proven leaders, good men, tested and proven. You have to know that."

"He's at odds with them. But they drew the line, not he. Yes, I've noticed the antagonism and, from all I can tell, he's absolutely on target on every issue. His grasp of the Scriptures at every point is vastly greater than theirs. They cite them from memory, he as though he'd written them himself."

"But between him and them there's more common ground than cause for conflict. You have to admit that. Both adhere to the Scriptures and both place high value on the circumspect life. They both love righteousness."

"There was a time I might have agreed with you, but that time has passed. No, I do not agree with you, Judas, not a single iota. Your exemplars of righteous living are power-loving peacocks that prefer lies to truth and pretense to common decency. They're forever posturing. They use the Scriptures to flail anyone and everyone who deigns to show them for what they are. And right now I'd say what they are is running scared."

Iscariot turns around to the Zealot for another shot. "Surely you see what I mean," he says, hands clinched and extended as if pleading.

"They bear the same message but are on parallel tracks, that's all. And, like paths in the desert, these lines will at some distant point merge into one."

"That's not an allusion or illusion I've so far encountered," Simon tells him.

"Whatever you think of them, the spiritual elite hereabouts are all that stand between us and the Romans."

"What they are is in bed with the Romans," Simon snaps back. "They're the Emperor's worker bees buzzing about to effect an atmosphere here of sweetness and light, keeping a lid on things so he can tax us blind. *Quid pro quo* it's called. 'You keep the order and we'll keep the change.'"

"Exactly my point," comes back Iscariot. "They do keep the order and that keeps the peace."

"Only if by keeping the order you mean intimidation."

"They're trying to do their best to maintain civility, and they're not bad people, Simon. They hold up standards and for the most part toe the mark at every point themselves. They know how things work."

"That they do. I'll give you that."

"Then why does he not hold out the olive branch to them?" Judas insists on knowing. "They can be assets, extremely valuable assets."

"Going around behind his back telling everybody he's a trickster and a charlatan? Not my idea of an asset. Telling them that seeing isn't believing after all? Writing off the most astounding things they've ever encountered as no more than coincidences? Accusing him of being a fake when they're the real fakes themselves? Hardly. Can you be so blind yourself, Judas, as not to see what's going on? These people are his sworn enemies, much more than the Romans are or probably ever will be."

"They're people he has to reckon with. Like it or not, they own the thoroughfares that lead to his kingdom."

"They own nothing he'll have need of. If anything, they're out there trying their best to block those thoroughfares you refer to. We saw above five thousand people fed to their gills on a handful of bread and fish. And what are they telling people? 'Nothing miraculous about that,' they say. 'Nobody goes hiking deep into the wilds without taking some snack along. Even if they're going no farther than Bethsaida they'll tuck away a loaf of bread. The kid got it started, and they all got into the act. Typical Galilean hospitality.' You've heard that one yourself, haven't you?"

Judas owns that he has.

"Some of them joked that the only miracle, given how prepared Galileans usually are, was that they didn't need oxcarts to haul away the leftovers. You've no doubt heard that one too."

No, he hasn't.

Thomas himself, he later tells Matthew, has little interest in the politics of Jesus' kingdom, "What's the point," he asks, "in being preoccupied with who's going to have this post and that in some kind of neo-Davidic monarchy until one's reasonably sure he's going to be in it? That to me is presumption squared."

"He did choose us for some specific purpose," Matthew reminds him.

"Yes, to go out and tell people about him and somehow explain his kingdom ethic to them, which so far we've miserably failed to do, largely because we hardly have a handle on it ourselves. We can't even explain who exactly he is, let alone whether the figures in his parables stand for specific things or categories of things or if sometimes they're simply literal."

"Over a period of time we do come up with a pretty good idea, don't we?"

"In some cases, yes, but there are still too many things we're still in the fog about. Exactly what and where his kingdom is—that's the one I can't seem to get a handle on. And faith. He requires faith in him. I do have faith in whatever he says. But faith *in* him—what's that? That he's the Christ? I do believe that, but there are things I don't grasp about it, things I get the feeling I should be grasping and he's personally holding me responsible for grasping."

Matthew nods. "I hear you. You're not in the soul-searching alone, Thomas. The word *faith* is as elusive as the word *love*. There are a hundred ways the word is used and for each of these a hundred shades and nuances. And on top of those another hundred ways it's simply misused. I think he wants us to believe in him the way we believe in God and then act accordingly. As I told you before, we believe something only when we behave as though it were true."

"Your little test does make sense, but a thorough grasp of the Christ still eludes me. Makes my head hurt to think about it. The man's an enigma. Beyond his being our lord and king someday, there isn't a great deal we know about him."

"There's a lot we know," Matthew argues. "There's magic in his touch—we know that. He has powers beyond those of any person we've ever known or known about. His heart reaches out to the sick and the maimed, the desperate, the unlovely, the despised, the poor, the forgotten, the little children, and all the other wretches atop the human refuse heap. We do know that much. He has an almost irresistible compassion for people our immediate world spits upon, at times quite literally."

"Like the people you had at your dinner that night?"

"Those certainly and the woman who anointed his feet and wiped them with her own hair and that man in the synagogue whose arm on the Sabbath he mended and our friend from Magdala."

"I hear what you're saying. But I guess what I most want to know, apart from his being the Christ, is who exactly he is. That's what has me stumped."

"I have every confidence that that too he'll reveal, but only when the time is ripe."

"What about us? Would you say then that we, you and I, are in the ranks of the reborn?"

"That's another thing that exists in my great personal store of ignorance. I honestly do not know. If it involves a ceremony or some other initiation of sorts, I'd have to say no, we're not. If it's tied to a rite of passage, again I wouldn't say so. If feeling comes into play, again no, at least not me. I don't know about you. But if it is entirely a matter of faith, which I'm beginning to think it is, then maybe yes, we're in that number."

"And the others, Peter and the other fishermen, the Zealot, Philip, Nathanael?" Thomas asks him. "And Judas Iscariot—do you think Judas is among the reborn?"

"I think that being reborn is probably an emerging process, a stepping-out point, just like being born in the first place. Exactly who has and who has not made it into this new plane of being I do not know. Nor do I think we should indulge in too much guesswork at that point. What I'm fairly certain of, however, is that any of us who have been born anew are still in a very early stage of infancy. Of that I am quite certain."

"And I don't even know that much."

"Do not flaunt your ignorance, good Thomas. It ill becomes you."

Another period of silence ensues. They and their companions are walking peripatetically toward a village to the north and west of Chorazin. For the most part, ambling in groups of two or three and occasionally four, their ranks are stretched out. Matthew and Thomas are invariably side by side, sometimes farthest away from Jesus himself and sometimes relatively close to him. Judas and the Zealot drop back or hurry forward to join them, singly at points and together at other points—the former invariably to theorize about his own role in Jesus' upcoming kingdom and the roles of Jesus' current enemies should he embrace them, and the latter ostensibly to hear what they have to say.

Simon the Zealot, having now broken from Judas' side, lags back and is soon beside them again. Although he holds his own with Iscariot, he listens rather than talks when around Thomas and Matthew. He is, in Thomas's estimation, every bit the revolutionary he has always been, but, agape over Jesus' incredible supernatural powers, he has shifted a full hundred and eighty degrees from the insurgent posture of his fellow Zealots of two years ago. Daggers have been replaced by visions of an unprecedented mass movement, which could require his own life rather than those of their conquerors and their minions. The man's idealism is beyond question.

"Should I call you Thomas or the Twin?" he asks, more to

120

initiate conversation, Thomas thinks, than check on his preferences. "Some of the fellows still call you the Twin."

"Their choice. What about Jesus? What does he call me?"

"Thomas."

"Let's follow his lead then on this as everything else. Good plan?"

The Zealot says yes, it is.

"If you slip, the Twin is okay. The more I think about it, there may be a lot of truth in that moniker. One side of me believes in the man with all my heart, whatever happens; the other side is obsessed with having everything make sense. I'm one of those little children he's forever going out of his way to cozy up to—bug-eyed and out of my tree with excitement. At the same time I'm bursting with more questions than all the Pharisees and theologians put together and am impatient to have them answered. I am two people, Simon. I think I really am."

"It's good to know both of you."

"Two people, mind you, not one person with two faces like the Pharisees and theologians hereabouts, who drip with piety in public but in private reek of treachery and are scheming against him, who broadcast rank lies as truth and who, I would not be surprised, are probably out there right now plotting his murder."

"Judas thinks he should be reaching out to recruit them."

"Judas might have a different view of Jesus' kingdom from the rest of us. He seems to look upon the Christ as a blown-up David without the first Lion of Judah's shortcomings, a monarch in the making, one with the might of Samson, the wisdom of Solomon, the justice of Samuel, and the lifetime of Methuselah all rolled up into one."

"He also thinks we might be off to Jerusalem again soon, this time for good."

"I can't argue one way or the other," Thomas replies. "Something does seem to be in the wind. Although Jesus' wonders become more and more astounding, he himself seems moodier than he used to be. Can see it in his eyes. Laughs less and smiles less. His brow's more frequently wrinkled, his head more downcast as he walks. There's not the spring in his step there used to be, not the same ring to his voice. Seems to be carrying a huge weight, greater than a body can bear, and he's struggling beneath it. Goes off to pray more, maybe to cry too—who knows. Sometimes downright morbid in things he says. And he seems to be in pain. All this when the crowds are getting bigger and bigger. Something's going on."

"Definitely I would say."

"Ever since returning from Tyre and Sidon, we seldom venture very far from the shores of Lake Gennesaret. A couple excursions to Magdala and Tiberias, but most of the time it's been in and about Capernaum. Bethsaida and Chorazin with some frequency, though seldom much further."

"More lively when he's surrounded by crowds."

"Right."

"And once he gets into a good story, he's all his old self, mugging and gesticulating the same as he always did."

"It's only around us he's sober and sullen."

"There's an urgency about him now. It's in his voice. There's an edge I can't remember being there before. He's more often than not curt with the Pharisees and theologians."

And so they talk as they once more enter the gates of the city. There, almost on cue to the Zealot's words, on hand to meet them are several of Capernaum's spiritual dignitaries. In costume and demeanor they might be mistaken for a welcoming delegation, but they clearly are not. Boldly they converge upon Jesus and his body of disciples and without prologue ask him for a sign from heaven to authenticate that he is indeed who the people are saying he is.

"You mean like a red sky at dusk being a sign of nice weather on its way and a red sky in the morning being a sign of stormy weather ahead? Is that what you mean by a sign?" Jesus asks them.

"Something like that," they say.

"Well, the signs in the sky and the signs of the times are two entirely different things," he tells them. "It is a perverse and faithless age that demands the sign you seek. It's not going to be given. The only sign that's forthcoming is the sign of Jonah. Enough said."

With that he turns around and, with his men about him, quickly exits the scene.

"The sign of Jonah?" the disciples are asking each other for the next several days. "What, pray, is the sign of Jonah?"

"Another metaphor," says Thomas.

Judas Iscariot, more visibly perplexed up until now by Jesus' behavior than any of his fellows, becomes strangely invigorated and upbeat. "He's going down for the next Passover. That's what it is. Has to be," he blurts out. "That's what's weighing on him. Just months away. Things'll start popping then. This may be the Passover to top all the Passovers, bigger than the original, who knows? No wonder he's lost in thought. For going on three years he's been simmering, simmering, and simmering. Now he's coming to a boil. All the pieces are about to fall into place."

"His triumph at last," opines one of the others.

"Triumph and enthronement," says Judas confidently.

"If that's the case, which indeed I truly hope it is," ventures Thomas, "it doesn't seem as though he anticipates an easy time of it. I see no unbridled joy in his brow, but I do have every intention of being at his side however the battle goes. Every day I know less than ever what his kingdom will be like, but I know more and more that I want to be in it."

"His kingdom is about to come!"

The kingdom of heaven and *eternal life*, terms used almost interchangeably by Jesus now, are themes he has broached in his preaching every day of late. His dominion, whatever its nature, seems as real and tangible to Jesus as the figs on the fig trees they pass every day or the sheep in distant pastures, but Thomas feels there is something missing in himself because it is nowhere nearly that real to him personally. It is still opaque at best and is fading from focus rather than becoming sharper. He cannot begin to imagine what it will look like or how it will be governed or exactly where it will be. Jesus goes on, however, talking about it as though it is patently the "pearl of great price" he referred to in one of his parables.

No one in the ranks of his disciples, however, asks their master the questions that have to be burning in their minds. No one is about to disappoint him or own to an ignorance of something others around them seem clearly to understand. Thomas wants to but is reluctant to sound contentious when everyone else is jubilant. Rather than ask what precisely the kingdom is, the men inquire about this detail and that in hopes of stumbling onto specific information, but that does not happen.

It is Judas Iscariot who one day asks Jesus, "Who's really going to be the greatest in the kingdom of heaven?"

Some children are playing in the vicinity where Jesus and his companions are standing when this question is posed. "Come over here," says Jesus to one of the little boys. The child drops what he is doing and comes immediately to the Nazarene's side. Jesus then positions the boy so that he is in the midst of the disciples.

"Let me tell you this," he says to his followers, "unless you change your perspectives and become like little children, you will never even enter my kingdom. Who will be greatest? The person who can be as humble as this little child—he, I tell you, will be the greatest in the Kingdom of God."

"How, pray tell, does a grown man become a little child?" Simon the Zealot asks Thomas later that day.

"I don't know," says Thomas. "Probably comes sometime after he's born again, I would guess. I suspect it's one more enigma we're expected to figure out, and there will be tons of disappointment if we don't."

"He does definitely like little children. The question is, what precisely is it about them that he likes so much? Their innocence? How they're so trusting? Their imaginations? Their candor? What?"

"As I said, I don't know. Could be faith again. He still talks a lot about faith."

It is at about this time that Jesus begins to tell his disciples about the days and weeks immediately ahead of them. "We will all be going into Jerusalem for the Passover," he finally tells them.

The disciples are moved to cheer, but the somber cast in Jesus' eyes and a note of resignation in his voice caution them not to. Each man moves in a step or two, tightening the arc about the Master. He looks each individual in the eye.

Thomas thinks he sees a tear. *For whom?* He wonders. *For himself or us?*

The men are motionless, they do not breathe.

"There I will endure not only a wealth of hostility from the Sanhedrin and Chief Priests and theologians but inordinate physical torment and anguish as well," he says, his eyes still fixed on those around him, his voice even more somber, almost sepulchral. "In the end, my friends, I will be killed. But on the third day after that I will be raised from the dead."

A collective audible gasp goes up from the disciples. They can neither comprehend nor believe the words they have just heard Jesus utter. They are stunned as though a sudden knife blade were driven into each of their hearts. It has to be hyperbole, thinks Thomas.

What's possessed him to say such a thing?

The stony silence is finally broken by Peter: "God forbid, Master, that any of this should happen to you!"

"Get out of my way, Satan!" Jesus, as if in pain, snaps back at him.

The big fisherman goes limp. His head droops and his hands dangle at his side.

"You're in my way, my dear, dear man. Don't you see?" Jesus then says, his voice now betraying anguish. "You're looking at things from a man's point of view, not God's."

Other disciples also step forth to protest this grim prophecy, but Jesus, as though trying to fend off a legion of devils, holds up his hands to halt them.

"If any of you wants to follow me," he declares, with chilling sobriety, "he must abandon all rights to his own life and take up his cross and go where I go. The man who's out to save his life will certainly forfeit it, and the man who gives up his life for my sake will find it. For what profit is there if a man gains the whole world at the price of his own soul? Is there a single thing a person could possibly offer to redeem his soul once he's lost it?"

No one says anything after that.

This is not the first time Jesus has prophesied his imminent death. Weeks earlier he did the same, but his tone then was more matter-of-fact, as though he were commenting on the weather or telling them they'd be taking a boat to somewhere across the lake rather than going by foot. It was easy for them then to dismiss any idea that he was actually going to die. To some it was almost a joke, as though he were injecting an irrelevancy into his discourse to see if they were paying attention, although no one laughed.

His declaration this time, in substance and brusqueness, cannot be taken lightly. It freezes them in place. They soon break company to go to the several places where they are going to spend the night.

"Sounds serious," says Levi Matthew. "Thinks he's going to be killed."

"What about the other half of his prediction?" asks Thomas. "On the third day—isn't that what he said—on the third day he would be raised from the dead?"

"I think that was it," replies Nathanael. "What of it?"

"Only that Jonah came out of the fish's stomach on the third day. He said something a bit ago about 'the sign of Jonah.' Remember?"

That's all that's said. Thomas and Matthew continue walking, neither of them breathing a word the rest of their way. It becomes a sleepless night for both. They do not know how much of what the Master has told them is meant to be taken literally and how much is contingent on conditions which may or may not actually occur. And there's still the remote possibility that it's some kind of a parable, a hypothetical horror story of sorts to make some point. If he is indeed serious about the first part, then he has to be serious about the second part as well. Trying to ponder that hurts Thomas's head yet more.

The previous time Jesus forecasted his death, the disciples, concluding it was merely a matter of rhetorical overkill, by the next morning could enjoy a good breakfast without undue anxiety. This time the better part of a week and much conversation among themselves pass before any of them seem comfortable and return to moods of high optimism again. Of the various and often dire predictions Jesus has made with respect to the immediate future, his mention that they will be going to Jerusalem for the Passover, still months away, is the only one they seem to look upon as a hard and fast certainty.

The uglier aspects of his prophecy, they concur, are doubtlessly provisional, depending on circumstances should his strategies fail, or simply as warnings reflective of his own dour mood of the moment. Considering the masses now behind him and the magnitude of his own powers, that he would actually be tortured and eventually killed is beyond their powers of imagination. Such anyway is Thomas's conclusion. This is not to say that a profound dread that the predicted events might actually happen does not exist deep in their individual psyches, but rather that such a fear, by its nature incomprehensible and thus incredible, has been so thoroughly repressed that not so much as a flicker penetrates the daylight of conscious thought.

Anxiety is in the air, though. They can all feel it. Something unthinkable has indeed taken root in their minds. Thomas, normally forever pressing for explanations of Jesus' parables and stories, has suddenly gone silent, and Peter, just in case, has taken to strapping on a short sword beneath his robe.

All the disciples find themselves scrutinizing the crowds for suspicious activity and people; and it is routine practice now that, once the crowd disperses, they whisk Jesus quickly off for the rest of the day to safe havens known only to a few. Simon the Zealot, onetime insurrectionist, is frequently looked to as the one to consult when matters of safety are of paramount concern.

There is much conversation about their trip to Zion, anticipated with no small excitement by some as the move that will put Jesus on his throne and them at his sides in administrative roles—and apprehensively by others, ironically, because of the personal risks he and they would be exposed to.

Judas Iscariot, Simon the Zealot confides to Thomas, cannot get to Jerusalem fast enough. Descending upon the Holy City at Passover time is consistent with their earlier vision of the Christ's triumphal entry into David's capitol, with endless undulations of humanity, like tidal waves, lifting him, driving him ever onward to his appointed destiny and his chosen disciples to theirs.

"It's an image I can embrace," says Thomas.

"But not one that Judas is as unambiguously elated over now as he was earlier," Simon tells him. "The thought that Jesus could possibly die stirs bad dreams, he says. These dreams erupt spontaneously like hiccups from deep within and intermittently throw a wet blanket over his joy. He's temperamental now in ways I don't think he ever was before. His favorite fantasy is under assault."

One day they are descended upon by a covey of children. Some are dressed in castoff clothing and are conspicuously ill-shod. Thomas sees Judas Iscariot react frenetically as though they are attacking him personally. He is a man in acute distress.

"Urchins!" the Judean says to no one in particular as he rushes toward them. "Urchins! Brought by mischief-makers to have the Master put his hands upon their heads to bless them."

"No!" says Jesus suddenly, when he sees what's going on.

Iscariot, caught up in his self-appointed mission, betrays no sign of hearing him. Politely and efficiently he goes about hurrying the little ones on their ways. "The Master's busy," he tells them. "Let's go, let's go. The Master's got lots of things to do today. We're preparing to go to Jerusalem soon. Thank you, thank you. Let's go."

"No!" says Jesus again, advancing toward the children to meet them. "Make way for these little fellows. Let them through, for of such is the kingdom of God."

Chastened, Judas draws back.

And the children, some of them barely big enough to walk, move in around Jesus. He reaches out and touches them, taking some of the smaller ones into his arms. Their eyes, wide and sparkling, never leave his face. They are as totally absorbed in him as he in them.

"They're enthralled by him," says the Zealot, standing next to Iscariot.

"And why would they not be?" Iscariot replies. "They know nothing of the paradoxes he embodies, nothing of his great and everlasting kingdom. For them it's sufficient to look up into his eyes and smile back at him when he smiles at them. To them he's a gentle, kindly father figure, little more."

"Let me tell you again," Jesus tells his companions. "Unless you become as one of these, you will never make it into the kingdom of God. And, furthermore, know this: The person who humbles himself and comes closest to one of these little ones, the same will be the greatest person in all my realm."

"Our great king," mutters Judas, "seems more anxious to be the king of children rather than men."

Before long, however, Jesus and his company are making their final preparations to leave Capernaum, maybe for good, to set out for Jerusalem. The Passover is still a ways off, but for some reason Jesus is set on being there months earlier in time for the Feast of the Tabernacle, then apparently to linger thereabouts until the greater holy day comes some time later.

On the very morning of their departure they are accosted by a young gentleman just inside the city gates. By his clothes and manners and soon by his speech, it is obvious that the man is well bred. Some of the disciples recognize him at once. They know him to be from one of the city's better families. He's educated, well-mannered, decent, and respectable in every way, the kind of young fellow any man could wish for a son.

He approaches Jesus in a humble manner and asks him, "Good master, what must I do to inherit eternal life?"

"Why do you call me good?" asks Jesus, almost as if in reprimand. "God is the only one who is good. If you want eternal life, keep the Commandments."

"Which ones?" asks the young man.

As he did earlier when a theologian asked him the same identical question, Jesus names the major Commandments: Do not kill; do not steal; do not commit adultery; do not bear false witness; honor your parents; and do not covet.

The young patrician nods affirmatively to each Commandment, beaming with relief in so doing. Smiling outright, he tells Jesus,

"All of these I have kept from my youth up. Is there anything else I must do?"

"Yes," Jesus answers, "there is one more thing. Go out and sell every last thing you own and give the proceeds to the poor. Then and only then come and follow me."

"This cannot be happening!" Judas whispers loudly to those about him. "He's asking the impossible! Look at this fellow. Just look at him. Look at him, will you! If ever there was a person you wanted in your kingdom, your camp, your anything, this wonderful young fellow is he. Money, ability, influence, character—he has it all."

The wealthy youth seems also to think Jesus is asking the impossible. His face suddenly falls; the heart seems to go right out of him. Downcast and disenchanted, the young man who has everything, as though wrongly dressed for a wedding feast, slowly walks away. Jesus has turned him away by demanding more of him than a human being could possibly be expected to give.

"Filthy lucre is not filthy," Judas Iscariot tells those close by, "if it does not stand between a man and God. Everybody knows that."

No sooner does the young gentleman disappear from their sight than Zebedee's wife, mother to James and John, comes hurrying toward them. She charges into their ranks to take her two sons by their hands to bring them to Jesus. Then, kneeling in front of the Nazarene, she looks straight up into his eyes. "A favor I have to ask of you, Savior of Israel," she says.

"And what is that?" Jesus asks her.

"These two sons of mine—might one sit at your right hand and the other at your left when you take your throne?" she asks him.

"I don't think you really know what you're asking," he replies. Then, looking first at James and then at John, he asks, "Can you two drink what I'm going to have to drink?"

"Yes," both respond as one, "yes, we can."

"Oh yes, you will indeed drink what I am about to drink, and I have already told you what that entails," he says somberly. "But as for sitting on either side of me, that is not something that's really mine to grant. Those positions belong to those to whom my Father has all along intended to award them."

Although for some time now the disciples have openly discussed their various roles of honor and responsibilities in the upcoming Kingdom of God, they are taken aback by the brazenness of Zebedee's two sons and their mother and seem about to give them the cold shoulder.

When Jesus takes note of this reaction, he holds up his hands to deter them.

"We all know that the Gentile kings lord it over their subjects and appoint tyrants under them that do the same. This is not how it's going to work with you," he tells them. "Oh no! In your cases anybody who aspires to greatness is going to have to play liegeman to all of the rest. If he wants to be top man, he must be everybody's slave—just as the Son of Man did not come to be served but to serve and to give up his very life for the freedom of others."

This puts the disciples back on common ground, albeit ground that is already beginning to shift beneath their feet.

By the time the company does finally leave the skyline of Capernaum behind them, the women and several others have joined them, including Mary, Jesus' own mother. With other family members from Nazareth, she has with increasing frequency been present on many of the occasions when Jesus has healed people and taught in the nearby towns and villages of Galilee. Now, on her own, she is determined to go with him, to witness triumph or catastrophe, into Judea.

Jesus says nothing to dissuade her.

Thomas and Matthew walk side by side. "What if he did do exactly what Jesus told him?" Thomas asks his friend.

"Who?"

"The young aristocrat who wanted eternal life. What if he immediately did go out and divest himself of all his wealth and gave all the proceeds to the poor and joined this train headed toward Jerusalem? Do you think that would have constituted the rebirth? That that would have put him on the path to the Kingdom of God?"

"Yes," answers Matthew without hesitation. "That would have demonstrated the level of faith Jesus seems to require. Faith is the key that opens the gate, and his doing precisely what Jesus told him would, to me anyway, be solid evidence that the man did have the required faith."

Boiling Plots

WHAT JESUS' DISCIPLES do not know right away upon passing through the Gate of Damascus into Jerusalem is that the Temple rulers, alert to the party's approaching the city, have been in session for several days now. The mindset of Judea's spiritual elite is different from that of their counterparts of Galilee, in that the Jerusalem elites have dismissed the fine details of Jesus' alleged miracles completely and have opted to go after the man himself.

"Wild, wild rumors have always drifted down from Galilee," their spokesmen have been saying, "so what is there to prove or explain? Simpletons have always believed the most absurd things. Jesus' being able to perform magic tricks is not what's at issue anyway. If he isn't an out and out charlatan, he's more likely to be in league with devils rather than in any way with God!"

Nicodemus, the young Pharisee who met with Jesus by night during his previous visit to the city, as a member of the deliberating body and firsthand witness to all that is said, is able to keep Jesus' sympathizers within the city abreast of the goings-on of the Sanhedrin. These fellow travelers in turn have been conveying the information, though not always in a timely fashion, to the Master's closest confederates.

The chief agitator, according to these reports, is Caiaphas, Chief Priest of the Temple in Jerusalem and presiding member of the Sanhedrin.

"By whose power does the man act?" Caiaphas is quoted as saying. "They are saying by God's. How else can he do the wonders credited to him? There is an answer to that, my good men. And we quake in our sandals at the very thought! Devils and demons are at work—unseen forces of evil we know to infest every corner of the world in which we live, bane of angels, enemies of the Most High!"

"Hear! Hear!" all his fellow Pharisees, save Nicodemus, called out in approval.

"Scrutinize the man's life, I say, before pronouncing him the conduit of God's grace. Is he seraph or sinner? Answer me that. One thing we do know, one thing that is certain, is that God does not empower sinners to do His work."

"Hear! Hear!"

Caiaphas' call to look hard at the man himself did make sense to Nicodemus, but the high priest's tone suggested clearly that he himself had already done all the hard looking he found necessary and had concluded that Jesus was something other than an angel. He had already made his own judgment—and, to Nicodemus's mind, without any obvious investigation whatsoever. The young Pharisee feared for the Galilean's life.

"He's an enemy of our faith and an enemy of Rome," the Chief Priest declared. "We have ordered our guards to take him into custody. He's too dangerous to be left on the loose."

"On what charge do we arrest him?" Nicodemus, suddenly finding his tongue, wanted to know.

"That he's the heart and soul of an insurgency and, ergo, an enemy of the people."

"Our intention, then, is to question him and hear him out?"

"It's to stop him," Caiaphas responded, "for the greater good. The man's a threat to our very existence. It is better that one man be sacrificed, should it come to that, than that the whole nation be destroyed."

The rest of the council nodded in somber agreement. "Hear! Hear!"

Thus, at the very hour the Nazarene and his party step foot into the city, Caiaphas's elite guards, heaviest of the heavies, are put on notice to take him at their first opportunity. Nothing is to be left to chance. Caiaphas has been adamant at this point. If the purported Christ is not stopped, he argued, the whole city will be in jeopardy.

Nicodemus' first impulse was to speak out against this action, but the lines of alarm and hate in the Chief Priest's brow dissuaded him from venturing a sound. He even had to stifle a cough. Never, since Nicodemus was first initiated into that body, had he seen the Sanhedrin so wrought up.

Thomas does not know what to credit Jesus' ensuing caution to—the young Pharisee's passing along of critical information or Jesus' own totally independent presentiments of what would surely come to pass. Assuming it is more likely the latter, he is, nevertheless, grateful that, needed or not, there are Judeans looking out for the Master.

Jesus is mobbed from the moment he first arrives in the Temple sector. Thomas can see Caiaphas's henchmen working in and out and through the crowd—brutish in size and aspect, as big as Peter some of them, others even bigger—knifing their ways into the front ranks, there to survey the routes that will best serve them to carry out their orders. They are clearly stymied and so simply stand there as if awaiting a signal of some sort to catapult them into action.

But there is no signal, and before long Thomas sees that they seem to be listening. He blinks, thinking this maybe to be no more than a trick of his own eyesight. It is not. The hulks are following what Jesus is saying. A few move in a step or two, but this apparently only so they can hear better. They're enthralled. *A new kind of miracle!*

In back of the crowd stands a man just inside the shadow of a portico. Throughout Jesus' discourse he does not move. Like a cleverly crafted statue, in stance poised as if to run should a threat arise, he stays frozen in place; only his eyes, darting to the left, then the right, then straight on and then quickly to the left again, assure Thomas that indeed he is a living being.

Presently, ending his homily with a parable, Jesus gives his disciples a nod and in an instant disappears into their midst, and the whole party retreats in the opposite direction from which they came, down a side street hardly wide enough for more than two to walk abreast. They pass the statuesque figure still in the portico's shadow. His eyes are no longer darting but fixed on the procession as they quickly exit. Now close-up, Thomas sees by the man's garb that he is a Pharisee and there is now a smile upon lips.

On his very first Sabbath in Jerusalem Jesus and his followers visit the pool of Bethesda near the Sheep Gate of the city proper. An angel of God, tradition has it, comes down from time to time to stir the waters of this pool; whoever first steps into it after the troubling of the waters will be healed of whatever disease he has. The feast-days are being observed, and so the five porticoes to the site are more crowded than normal with invalids and the families of invalids trying to get to poolside.

There happens to be a man there whose legs have been paralyzed for almost forty years. How long he's been lying there nobody knows, and, from all appearances when the visitors come upon the scene, nobody cares. Everyone is preoccupied either with himself or with his own relatives. The poor old wretch has nobody.

Jesus stops in front of him and asks, "Are you hoping to be healed?"

"There's no one to help me into the pool when the waters are troubled," the old man tells him.

"Not to worry. You don't need those waters," says Jesus, with a smile. "Just pick up your bed and walk. Go ahead. Try it."

Without hesitation or a second thought, the poor soul does as Jesus commands him. His limbs are suddenly as healthy as anyone's; his pallet under his arm, he practically dances out into the street. The disciples note the glint in their master's eyes as he continues to smile at the old man disappearing into the crowd. On a whim Thomas follows the onetime street beggar for a short while as he skips down the street with his pallet under his arm.

The man soon encounters a group of Pharisees. "Hey, you, it's the Sabbath," shouts out one of them. "Don't you know it's a violation of the holy day to go around lugging your bed like that?"

"I've just been healed!" the old fellow chirps back at him. "My healer said, 'Pick up your bed and walk.' And that I did, and he was right. See for yourself. I'm actually walking."

"And who might your healer be?"

"I really don't know. He's back there in the crowd."

The Pharisees, knowing right well who the healer has to be, quickly descend upon Jesus to reprimand him for breaking the Sabbath. "You yourself break the Sabbath by healing this man and then compound that by telling him to carry his bed down the streets, making him a Sabbath-breaker like yourself," one of them accuses him. "Have you no respect for the Law?"

"My Father does his work and, therefore, I will do mine as well," Jesus responds.

"By 'Father' do you mean God? If so, not only do you violate the Sabbath, but you blaspheme. In calling God your own father, you put yourself on a level with Him."

Storming out of his presence, they are now as adamant as Caiaphas that the man's lips must be sealed one way or another. Jesus' latest feat of healing the paraplegic has them in a dither. The wretched man in question has been of no help; it does not matter to him that his cure may have resulted from a profanation of the Sabbath or that the circumstances surrounding the miracle are suspicious at best. His going about the streets with his pallet under his arm telling his story to any and all who will listen is finding more credence than the Pharisees' postulation that the powers of darkness no doubt played a much bigger role in the phenomenon than those of light.

As the festivities surrounding the Feast of the Tabernacle near their peak, Jesus goes into the Temple and holds forth, expounding the Scriptures and telling the people truths he has so far only shared with his disciples. His audience is taken by his air of authority and by the profundity of what he says.

"How does he know so much?" ask some of the people in amazement. "By whom and when was he taught?"

Jesus hears this and answers, "My teaching is not mine but his who sent me. A person who speaks on his own is only trying to puff himself up. But if someone is really out to glorify God, mark that person. He's the one you should listen to. What he tells you is most likely to be true."

"The Law of Moses is the only truth!" shouts out a Pharisee to him.

"You dare claim the Law of Moses!" Jesus retorts, shaking his finger at the Pharisee and the theologians about him, his eyes boring straight into their ranks. "Not a single one of you obeys it!"

They throw up their hands in denial.

"If you do," he asks, "why then are you plotting to kill me? Is it because, as you say, that I violate the Sabbath? You tell people that Moses commanded circumcision, which, by the way, he did not—circumcision preceded Moses. But be that as it may, you say that, if the infant boy's eighth day falls on the Sabbath, then it's all right to go ahead and circumcise him on the Sabbath. Then you turn around and fault me for healing some wretched, suffering human being on the Sabbath. You must learn to distinguish the substance of the Law from the highlights that just happen to catch your eyes."

This causes a rumbling from the people. Some call out, "He is surely a prophet!"

"Not just a prophet," say others, "but indeed the Christ also!"

Still others argue, "No, he can't be the Christ. You can tell by his accent that he's from Galilee, and the Scriptures say the Christ will come from the city and lineage of King David, which means he will come from Bethlehem, the city of David."

"Is that so?" Thomas asks of Levi Matthew when later they are alone together.

"Yes. I told you there was something about his birth that didn't quite square with what I knew of the prophecies."

Thomas remembers. "Then how do you reconcile that now?" he asks.

"There is no longer anything to reconcile. I broached the question with his mother. She said he was born not far from where we are right now, in Bethlehem, just as the Prophets had predicted, during the big census-taking under the reign of the first Caesar."

"I could wish that all issues surrounding him were so easy."

"Like, why then is he stalked like an arch-criminal in the city of his birth?"

"Not what I was thinking. He was an arch-criminal in the town where he grew up too, you'll remember. No, what I mean is, like, where and what exactly is his kingdom? The Christ has always been touted as being the Savior of Israel. The Master apparently needs to be saved *from* Israel. So whom exactly then is he supposed to save? And from what or whom? And, for that matter, how? The very people who should be waving his banner are the ones trying to kill him. And what is to be our role in all this? What did he pick us for? Not to be viceroys or governors certainly, as friend Judas seems to think. We can't even go out and explain his gospel to fishers and goatherds without stumbling all over the place. We don't know where we're going or why we're here. For every question he answers, two rise up to take its place. How does a man go about being born again? He tells us God is our father. How so?"

"And what is the great, vast, unfathomable God like? You left out that one, Thomas. And is it possible that we can even have glimpses of Him?"

"He calls Him his father. Maybe he himself is our one big glimpse, Levi. The problem there, of course, is that he's like nobody or nothing we've ever known."

"We'll have to ask him sometime about that, don't you think?"

While Thomas and Matthew continue to ponder the imponderable, the Temple rulers, so far foiled in their attempts to take Jesus and now bitten to the quick by his accusation that they are plotting his assassination, gather at their quarters to contemplate their next action. They are aquiver with rage and confusion because, momentarily at least, by striking at the very root of their pride, the Nazarene has put them on the defensive. Again the young Pharisee Nicodemus is witness to their deliberations.

Hastily convening, they press their guards to take immediate action. Irrespective of where Jesus is or who he is with or how many are with him, the rulers want him bound and forthwith brought before them. Having so ordered their men, they retire to their chambers to await the guards' return. All of them, the disciples are later informed, are tense and on edge.

Annas and Caiaphas, the Chief Priests, pace frantically about, all the time grumbling under their breaths, "Why don't they come?"

Nicodemus wonders the same thing, though for his own reasons. Calm on the surface, he feels a fire raging within. From his first meeting with Jesus the young Pharisee has held out for the possibility that the strange Nazarene may indeed be the Christ. That he is a Galilean and quite obviously holds the Pharisees in contempt gives Nicodemus pause to wonder. But in all else the man from the north seems like a true prophet.

Suddenly there is a noise at the door. Nicodemus is the one who reaches over to unlatch it. And there stand the Sanhedrin's special officers—alone. They simply stand there, not the hard, coarse-featured, weathered men the council commissioned to take Jesus in hand.

Oh, they are the same men all right, but there is very little of the earlier rawness—their officious demeanor and swagger of borrowed importance. There's an air of gentleness about them now. They seem to be held in ecstatic trance. And for one of the few times in his life Nicodemus thinks he can read happiness in men's faces. The thought begins to excite him.

"Why haven't you brought him?" calls out Caiaphas.

"Have you been fooled too?" shouts another Pharisee. Getting no response from the officers, he suddenly turns around and, making a sweep of his hand, says, "They believe in him! They actually do! And how about you, my fellow Pharisees? Do any of you believe in him too?"

Nicodemus slowly steps forward. "Let us be fair," he begins. "Our law does not permit us to condemn a man to death without first hearing his side and determining what exactly he has and hasn't done."

"Aha, are you too a Galilean?" asks a man accusingly.

Then, not giving him time to respond, others quickly rattle off arguments he has now heard dozens of times. Did not Jesus intentionally violate the Sabbath and teach others to do so also? And did he not put himself on a plane with the Lord God Jehovah by calling him his father? Does he not continually traffic with sinners of the rankest order and at the same time declare the most upstanding of men to be a generation of vipers? Is he not the very antithesis of the true Christ?

Then it is that Caiaphas himself steps forth. "Is not this man an insurrectionist who, sooner or later, will bring down the full fury and might of the Roman Empire against us?" he says. "That is the big question we have before us. Has the lesson of the Baptizer been lost on you men?"

"Lesson of the Baptizer?" Nicodemus answers back. "The Baptizer did not incur the fury of the Roman Empire. Only that of Herod's harlot. And that fury came down on John alone, no one else. There is no indication that the Romans in the least are worried about this Galilean—none I know of and none you know of either. The only thing he's done to the Romans so far has been to heal the slave of one of their own centurions."

"Let the Romans hear people saying he's the Christ. That'll get their attention," the Chief Priest shoots back.

"He does have their attention. Herod knows what they're saying about him. And he isn't on his high horse. Nor have we seen any of Pontius Pilate's men milling about trying to shut him up. Pilate has to know about him too."

"But we all know how quick the Romans have been in the past to come down on would-be Christs. And some of the blame always rubs off on us, because we're supposed to control our own people," snaps Caiaphas.

His minions call out, "Hear! Hear!"

"And how, pray tell, can we control them if someone's out there always undermining our authority and whipping them up to mob frenzy?"

"But what if he is the Christ, Caiaphas?" Nicodemus then asks. "What if it turns out that the rumors are on target? What then?"

That is the moment, Nicodemus will one day be telling men of a different, kinder perspective, that marks the beginning of his slow withdrawal from the company of his fellow Pharisees,. No longer will the overseers of public welfare trust him. Thereafter he will often notice them whispering in hushed tones so he cannot hear them. Where Jesus is concerned they will leave him out of their plans almost completely.

For this reason the disciples are not forewarned two days later of the trap the Temple elders are about to set for Jesus. In the end, however, it makes no difference. The Master is quite equal to the occasion.

Jesus arrives at the approach to the Temple early. Soon a crowd gathers about him, and he sits down to teach them. He stops in mid-sentence when suddenly interrupted by a loud commotion in the street. In no time at all a group of Pharisees and theologians arrive on the scene, half dragging and half pushing a woman in their direction. The crowd opens up to let them through. The men head straight for Jesus and cast the woman at his feet. No one has to say what she is. Everyone seems to know. They have all seen her likes many times at the agora, in a doorway, or at a window. She is the symbol of everything that disgusts them, the very picture of license and debauchery; she is the filth and vomit of the street.

"Rabbi," her captors say, "this woman has been caught in the very act of adultery. Moses commanded that her kind should be stoned. Now what do you say?"

This is obviously a very simple trap. Thomas knows it right away and so also apparently does Jesus. If Jesus commands her to be stoned, the Romans will surely arrest him for complicity in murder. If not, the Pharisees will have the people upon him for disregarding the Law of Moses. An almost classic dilemma.

At first Jesus ignores them and, bending down, begins to draw characters in the dirt. Finally looking up, he says, "Let the one of you who has not sinned cast the first stone." He thereupon goes back to his writing.

The oldest Pharisee in the group hangs his head and starts making his way back through the crowd. Some of the younger theologians stoop as if to pick up stones, then stay their actions and follow the older men in solemn procession away from Jesus. Soon they are all gone.

"Did no one condemn you?" Jesus, looking up again, asks adulterous woman.

"No one, lord."

"Then neither do I. Go your way and sin no more."

"Did he endorse her immorality or simply rebuke her accusers?" Thomas asks Levi Matthew as they leave the Temple precincts.

"Principally the latter would be my guess," says Matthew.

"Mine too, but he seems to have totally dismissed her offense."

"He called it sin. 'Sin no more,' he told her. What struck me was that he put their sins on the same or maybe even on a more serious level than hers. Sins of the flesh are bad, but sins of hate and malice and incomparable arrogance are apparently more egregious. Men playing God are the most reprehensible of sinners. I think he holds out more hope for her than for them."

"He is getting harder and harder on them."

"As they on him. Iscariot might see it differently. I only hope it does not end badly."

Flight into Perea

WITH EVERY DAY now there is duel of wits. And at every day's end Jesus' pious antagonists exit the scene with heads down and shoulders bent, the fringes of their tightly woven robes brushing the paving stones as they work their ways back to the Temple to work out scenarios for their next encounter. And the following day the crowds are bigger than they were the day before.

By week's end, however, rather than face off against Jesus in the streets, the Pharisees and theologians switch to a different strategy. Suddenly all smiles and sunshine, they invite their nemesis and his disciples to a dinner to be held at the home of one of their richest and most prestigious members. It is a ploy, of course, that all the disciples realize from the start.

"What they want to do is draw Jesus into a situation in which his flagrant disregard for tradition is put on exhibition in a milieu wherein he has no gallery to play to, one in which they will have the upper hand and can embarrass and humiliate him at their pleasure," Matthew tells Thomas .

"Visions of leading him into the lion's den cavort in their heads."

"More or less. What they're really doing is bringing the lion into their sheepfold. Not only are they not as holy as they comport themselves to be, but it turns out now they aren't as clever either. I strongly doubt if roast lamb is all that's on their menu."

Judas does not see it that way. "They're holding out the olive branch," he breaks in. "Always just a matter of time. He may yet discover their true value."

"He's long since discovered that," Matthew tells him.

Jesus politely accepts the invitation on behalf of them all.

And so it is that Jesus and his followers go to dine with the

Pharisees. Also present at this meal are a fair number of theologians. In the foyer to the dining room there is a basin of water and a towel. Having washed and tidied themselves prior to leaving for the dinner, however, Jesus and his company amble on past the water and towel and take their seats. As soon as they do so, as if on cue, the dignitaries, already seated, glance in great horror to their host, whose face registers equal chagrin.

"You didn't wash!" he snaps, bolting to his feet. "What are you? Pagans?"

"Should have guessed as much," growls another Pharisee.

"Apparently another tradition you've elected to trample under foot," a third accuses him.

"Which is all it is," replies Jesus, "a tradition you made up yourselves for the express purpose of parading yourselves to be more righteous than other men. My word, one would think I'd just smashed the tablets Moses brought down from Sinai or rent the veil of the Holy of Holies. You're forever making up things. This cleansing you so insist upon is not prescribed by Moses and certainly not by God."

"Better to err with too much cleansing than too little," the host throws back at him.

Jesus stands to answer. To Thomas, now sitting directly across from him, he suddenly seems bigger than life. The muscles of his face and throat tighten. His eyes narrow and then widen. And, when he speaks, his voice sounds like a blast from heaven. For more than two years now a storm has been gathering and now is about to break. Thomas feels it in his bones.

"Oh yes," Jesus retorts, "you Pharisees are so big on cleaning the outsides of things, cups and dishes and such. But you know what? Inside you're saturated with maliciousness and greed. You shallow, blockheaded miscreants, it is not what touches a man's mouth that makes him unclean but what's already in his heart and mind. From a person's mind is evil born: murder, theft, lasciviousness, perjury, and blasphemy. These are what sully him, make him vile, not his eating without washing his hands."

"Best it is to be circumspect about everything!" counters his host.

"Curses upon you then! Curses upon you Pharisees!" Jesus cries out. It is not rage Thomas hears in Jesus' voice so much as disgust, very heavy disgust. "Oh my yes, you're circumspect all right—about some things. You measure out your tithe of mint and your tithe of aromatic leaf flecks and your tithe of assorted herbs right down to the last teensy-weensy grain. But you're utterly oblivious to the weightier issues of justice and mercy!

"Curses upon all of you Pharisees! For what you most relish are seats of honor in the synagogues and having everybody bow and scrape to you in public places.

"Curses upon you! You insufferable, miserable pretenders! You're like whitewashed sepulchers—spotlessly clean and lovely on the outside but on the inside steeped in putrescence and dead men's bones."

It is at this point that one of the theologians springs abruptly to his feet. "Sir!" he shouts at Jesus, "when you hurl insults at these men, you should know you're insulting us as well!"

"Quite correct," answers Jesus, glaring at the man. "Yes, you are absolutely correct. You are of the same cloth, are you not? And so don't think for one instant I would not include you. Oh no, not you peacocks of theology! Never! Not for the world would I leave you out. So I say curses upon you theologians too, for you heap upon men's backs burden upon burden of hairsplitting details and lift not one finger to help them bear them.

"Curses upon you theologians too, for you piously erect memorials for martyred prophets—prophets, incidentally, that your own predecessors murdered. They slaughtered them and you memorialize them! What hypocrisy! Let me tell you that the blood shed by all of these men of God from Abel on down will be on the hands of this generation!

"Curses upon you theologians, for you have confiscated the keys to the Kingdom of God put in your trust. You've not been able to enter that kingdom yourselves and so have slammed shut and locked its doors to everybody else. Curses on you especially for that!"

Having said these things, Jesus signals his companions and takes quick leave of the Pharisee's table. The Pharisees and theologians, faces ruddy and eyes ablaze with hate, remain there long after their company has left, nursing their wounds and devising fresh schemes whereby they might trip Jesus up and lay him open to ridicule before the people.

By the next day, however, the men from the north have disappeared. The evening seems to have whisked them all away. The Sanhedrin's plan was to convene that following morning to devise new strategies by which to take Jesus, but by first light he is gone, he and the whole company he brought from Galilee. Completely disappeared. No sightings of them on the roads leading to the north, none on those to the west that intersect other northerly routes. Not a soul in the city who will, or even can, point to the direction they took. Vanished.

Some Council members take heart in this. They strut about the Temple precincts with a new spring in their steps. There is a fresh lilt in their voices as they greet one another at the portals or near the Holy of Holies. Nicodemus shares their delight, though for entirely different reasons. He does not know where Jesus has gone but does know men who do.

Others evince caution, including Caiaphas and his father-in-law Annas, the High Priests. Plotters themselves, they worry about what new plots the Nazarene might be instigating in absentia . . . or maybe just in hiding. The Passover, when the city will be bursting beyond its bounds with pilgrims, is yet three months away. Is their nemesis out there now, they wonder aloud, scheming their overthrow on that occasion? One cannot rule out anything. Paranoia has a stranglehold on them.

Nicodemus, alienated from his fellows but not quite ready to align himself with Jesus, is simply relieved that the Galileans are safely wherever they are. The crisis he deemed inevitable has been averted. For the time being anyway.

It is to Perea eastward beyond the River Jordan, where over a thousand years earlier the children of Reuben and Gad and half the tribe of Manasseh had settled, that the folks from Galilee, with not a few newcomers to their ranks from Jerusalem, have taken themselves. Once across the river, they proceed at a more relaxed pace.

"That bordered on the exhilarating," says Matthew to Thomas, "his calling down the theologians, I mean."

"He has no time for them."

"And shouldn't have. They are forever trying to squeeze the great and everlasting God, in whose mind we live and move and have our being, into a box. They'll agree that He has to be vast far beyond our powers to comprehend, but then they'll proceed to break Him down into vague attributes, which are no more than high-sounding words void of clear reference, and expostulate on those alleged attributes like they were concrete realities. The very word 'theology' means 'the science of God.' They really believe, Thomas, they've got God all pinned down. The audacity of it!"

"I take it you've never been one of their fans."

"Don't get me started."

"You're already started. I see where you're going, but would deeply appreciate a more detailed map."

"They will tell you about His holiness, totally unaware of the redundancy of it all. We use the word 'holy' to refer to whatever pertains to God, whatever is especially His. To say He is holy is to say He is godly. They say He is just, which means He measures up to some vague abstract notion of justice, then reinvent whatever that is to fit given circumstances. He can never do what He wants to do, but is driven this way and that by one or more of His attributes: in some instances He is conflicted because one attribute's pushing and another's pulling. They are little men with little minds but look upon themselves as intellectual giants."

"Did any of your apparent disgust for them push you into becoming a publican?"

"Not consciously, no. It did make me feel like the odd man out, and maybe that influenced me to step out of the mainstream. That's a possibility, but I didn't do it to spite anyone. I feel reasonably certain of that."

"Jesus seemed particularly critical of their applications of the Laws of Moses."

"And should have been. Personally I think he was a little soft on them at that point," Levi tells him. "Again they have a bunch of big sweeping principles: Keep the Sabbath, don't kill anybody, honor you mother and father, don't steal, don't adulterate and so on. They've taken it upon themselves to break these down into ten thousand different applications and have had the nerve to say this or that is what God meant by such and such and so and so. Walking, for example, they say is working, which it probably is to them. Therefore, you can walk only so far on the Sabbath before you cross the line called **SIN**. Doesn't matter how long or short your legs are, whether you simple enjoy a good stroll, or whether the sheep break out of the fold and scatter. They make up rules for everything under the sun and represent them as divine truths."

"How do they break up the last of Moses' Commandments: Thou shalt not covet?"

"They don't. That's where they live and how they do their business. That one Commandment for the most part they leave alone and simply ignore. To them it can't be codified; it involves state of mind, as we've already agreed, and is therefore elusive. You can't measure it or weigh it or by any device known to man discern its density or presence."

"What purpose do all their petty legal distinctions serve then?"

"Only to delineate the righteous from the unrighteous and the ultra-righteous from the just barely righteous—themselves primarily from everybody else. It has everything to do with social posturing and virtually nothing to do with moral character. Their minds aren't big enough to handle abstractions, so they focus on things that can be quantified, picayune things the Scriptures might mention in passing—not the moral principles hammered upon time and time again. They dwell on ceremonies of their own making and the outward trappings of moral living and dismiss completely such matters as justice, mercy and truth."

"All of which, of course, make Jesus a hugely threatening

personality. If he comes from God, they are indeed both damned and stripped of purpose—and livelihood too for that matter. Makes you pity the poor souls."

"Speak for yourself, Thomas. I have suffered their judgment all my life and seem to have run clean out of pity."

It is only days before Jesus has gathered a substantial following in Perea as well. Word of him has preceded his actual coming, and so the people are ready to hear him. For a brief while to the disciples it is old times again such as they knew in Galilee: No conspirators out to trap him in the towns of Perea, no instances of their quickly evacuating a location because behemoth Sanhedrin hirelings might break through to manhandle him, no one to twist what he says into something entirely different. He is comfortable here and so are those in his entourage. He's back to teaching with stories and parables, largely uninterrupted, as was the case in Capernaum.

And the people listen.

"There once was a man," on one occasion he tells his listeners, "who had two sons, the younger of whom came to his father one day and asked for his whole inheritance up front. The father sadly obliged him, and he left the farm immediately to spend all of his wealth on strong wine and wanton women and all manner of riotous living. When his last shekel was spent, a famine came upon the land of his exile and he found himself in desperate straits.

"His only recourse was to hire himself out to a hog farmer who needed someone to swill his swine. He had absolutely no money and was so hungry at times he was tempted to dish up some of the swill for himself.

"It was then he came to his senses and cried out loud, 'Why, my father's hired hands have all they need to eat and more, and here I am literally starving to death! What I'll do is go back to my father and tell him that I have befouled myself in his and Heaven's eyes and am no longer worthy to be called his son. And I will ask him, please, to take me on as a hired hand. That's what I'll do.'

"And he did. He left the hog farm and the country he was in and headed back home. When he first appeared on the horizon, his father saw him and his heart seemed to rise into his throat so that he could not even speak. He ran to his son, faster than he ever thought he could, and threw his arms around his neck and hugged him tight to himself and kissed him.

"The son slowly pulled away and, hanging his head, said, 'I have done evil in Heaven's eyes and yours and am not worthy to be called your son. . . .'

"He would have gone on, but his father stopped him and called out to his servants, saying, 'Quick! Go get some good clothes, the best we have, for him to put on! A ring for his finger and sandals for his feet! Hurry, hurry! And kill the fatted calf, for we're going to celebrate as we have not celebrated in a long time. This is my son! I thought he was dead, but he lives. I thought he was lost, but now he is found!'

"And so the celebration began.

"All this time the older brother had been toiling in his father's fields. When he neared the house at the end of his workday, he heard music being played and the sound of people dancing and laughing. 'What's going on?' he asked one of the household servants.

"'Your younger brother has come home,' the servant told him, 'and your father has killed the fatted calf to celebrate his safe return.'

"This made the older brother so furious that he would not go into the house but stayed outside and seethed in his anger. Soon his father came out and asked him to come in. 'Look,' his older son, quivering with emotion, erupted, 'for years I have worked like a slave for you. Not once have I ever disobeyed you or given you cause for sorrow. And in all that time you never gave me so much as a lamb that I might provide a feast for my friends. Now this wastrel brother of mine comes back after spending half your substance on trollops and drunken revelry, and for him you kill the calf I helped to fatten!'

"'My son, you've been with me right along,' the father tries to explain. 'Everything I have is yours. But for this we just have to celebrate! This is you brother! I thought he was dead, but he's alive! I thought he was lost, but now he's found! Don't you understand?'"

"Okay and then what?" asks a man in the audience.

"Then nothing. That's the end of the story."

"Not a good story," says another man, this one a Pharisee. "The elder brother got the short end. It wasn't fair."

"It isn't a story about fair and unfair," Jesus tells them. "It's about a father, not a judge. About a father's love for his son. You need to know how much a father loves his son. That's very, very important."

There is a catch in his voice, Thomas notes, when he says this.

A few days later in another town he tells his audience a story about a great landlord who went about settling accounts with his overseers. One of the overseers, it so happened, came up ten thousand denarii short of what he owed the landlord. "I have no money with which to repay you," the man told his master.

"Then you will have to be sold into slavery, you and your wife and your children, and the proceeds of that sale will go toward your debt," the lord ordered.

The overseer then slumped to his knees before his lord. "Please be patient with me!" he pled, weeping all the while. "I will pay you back. Give me time before you do this awful thing."

Moved with pity for the man, his master finally said, "I will do better than that. Your debt to me is hereby canceled. You and your family are free to go."

Once this same overseer returned to the estate he managed, he quickly looked up a man who worked under him who owed him a denarius. That's right—a single denarius. He then literally grabbed the fellow by his shirt collar and demanded, "Pay me what you owe me! And pay me now!"

"I don't have the money," said the laborer on his knees, begging. "Please be patient. I'll need a little bit of time."

But the overseer gave him no time. He had the laborer immediately seized and thrown into prison until he came up with the pittance he owed him. The imprisoned man's fellow laborers looked on in horror and went to the overlord and told him exactly what happened. Before long the master called the overseer back into his presence.

"You despicably vile manager!" said the master. "Didn't I forgive you your debt when you begged me to do so? Shouldn't you, then, have taken pity on your poor laborer the same as I, your lord and master, did to you?"

And so it was that the great landlord, filled with anger, had his officers lay hands upon the ungrateful rogue and drag him off to prison—there to remain until he paid back every denarius he owed him.

"Take heed," the Nazarene warns, "lest you be that man."

Miracles are sparse. Thomas finds this curious. Healings do occasionally happen but, as opposed to those in Galilee and Jerusalem, they occur almost exclusively when people go to Jesus and ask him for specific help. He no longer needs to establish himself. All Israel knows who he is. Any kindnesses now are just that—kindnesses. He simply cannot say no to a sufferer in need of his mercy.

Weeks turn into months. As in Galilee, the crowds get larger as he moves on from one town to the next, and the numbers of those now following him wherever he goes likewise grow. In Jerusalem, the disciples learn, the lines of alarm in the faces of the Jewish Council, which convenes almost daily, are also growing. Caiaphas and Annas are frantic. They are preparing against his imminent return.

As the time of the Passover draws closer, so also, according to reports that are coming into the city, seem to be Jesus and his masses. When he crosses the Jordan back into Judea at Jericho, word of the event reaches the Sanhedrin by early afternoon of the day it takes place. By the frenzied reaction of the Pharisees and the theologians upon hearing this, one might think that the walls of the ancient metropolis have come tumbling down once more and that the tremors are threatening to bring down the ramparts of Jerusalem with them. Twice the Council meets that day, once at first word and again when eyewitnesses arrive in the Holy City with specific details.

Not since the days of Joshua has Jericho been taken so by storm. The first stir comes before Jesus even steps inside the gates of the city. It seems that a blind man by the name of Bartimaeus is sitting on the side of the road near the gates when the Galilean is about to pass through them.

"Who comes?" the street beggar calls out.

"Jesus the Nazarene," someone tells him.

The name immediately sparks recognition. Bartimaeus's face lights up. "Jesus, Son of David, have mercy upon me!" he shouts. "Make me to see again."

To this Jesus responds kindly, "Then I say, 'Open your eyes and see.' Your own faith, my dear fellow, has healed you."

And a miracle transpires in an instant. The man looks up wide-eyed and quickly turns to look around in every direction, then leaps up as though shot from a catapult and races on ahead of Jesus and his company into the city, trumpeting loudly as if in disbelief, "I can see! I can see! Can you believe it? I can see!"

If there is a soul in Jericho who has not already heard about the Nazarene and his powers before this, it can be safely said that by the time he and the gathering masses about him advance so much as a furlong into the city's main corridor every last person residing therein knows who he is and what he's just done.

Great crowds jam the roadway toward the marketplace. From everywhere men, women, and children descend upon the scene. From their shops and stores, from their kitchens, from their nests of idling and frivolity, from their sickbeds it seems also, they come. One would not think there are so many people in all of Jericho.

Throngs line either side of the agora approach. The first ranks are filled by early comers and those who manage to pick their ways to the front, many of whom are respected elders deferred to by neighbors and relatives but not a few wiry adolescents whose elbows find the seams. Then there is a tier of taller people and those who make themselves so by standing tiptoed and stretching, and behind them mothers and fathers with children on their shoulders.

Advancing slowly because of the crowds, the Galilean and his train presently come upon a place where there is a sycamore tree a short ways back from the thoroughfare. Clinging to a branch halfway up the tree is a man leaning streetward. He goes unnoticed by the horde of onlookers but apparently not by Jesus. He is a short man and, by his attire, likely a publican.

When the Nazarene comes even with the sycamore, he suddenly

stops and looks straight up at the almost comical figure in the tree. Others follow his gaze. A man from the crowd immediately grabs Jesus' arm, apparently to alert him to the status of the fellow in the branches so the celebrated stranger need not be bothered by him.

Ignoring the man's caution, Jesus calls up to the publican by name. "Zacchaeus," he says, "hurry up and come down. I'd like to be a guest in your house today."

The man, whose name indeed is Zacchaeus, comes clambering down, dangling momentarily from the bottommost limb, then drops the rest of the way to the ground.

The fellow beside Jesus is still clutching his arm. "He's a cursed publican, can't you tell that?" he exclaims excitedly, loudly. "He's a sinner! Have nothing to do with him. He's a sinner!"

"He's going to a sinner's house," some voices around them begin to chime in.

And then, as a tossed pebble sends ripples farther and farther out into a still pond, wave upon wave of voices send the message to the far fringes of the crowd: "He's going to a sinner's house, he's going to a sinner's house, he's going to a sinner's house."

Once on firm ground, Zacchaeus the publican stands before Jesus, his head bowed, trying not to look fully into the Nazarene's face. "For you, oh Lord," he vows, "half my wealth shall I give to the poor. And if by fraud I have robbed any man, I shall repay him four times over." Then and only then does he slowly look up.

"Today," cries out Jesus, loudly enough for all about to hear, "I say salvation has come to this man's house. He too is a true son of Abraham."

"He's a sinner, he's a sinner!" voices are still protesting.

"It is sinners," Jesus shouts back to them, "whom the Son of Man has come to seek and to save!"

When the Pharisees and theologians of Jerusalem learn of the Galilean's closing in on their city and of the reception he is getting en route, they take counsel together to devise strategies by which they can draw the Romans into their cause. This is made known to Jesus and his comrades on a daily basis by friends from inside the Hoy City, one of them a Pharisee himself.

They are in no particular hurry and so there is ample time to talk on the road. "Why do you think he's gone to calling himself the Son of Man?" Thomas asks of Matthew.

"To identify with us I suppose," his friend speculates. "To let us know he's not some other kind of being. I don't really know. He's the most extraordinary man that ever lived—we can agree on that—but a man nonetheless."

"He says it's sinners he's come to save. What's your take on that? Does he not look upon us all as sinners?"

"I'm sure he does. He's being ironic in a way. Some of us know we are and are appropriately weighed down by the fact; others go on their merry ways thinking they're a cut above the rest and so consequently, by comparison, are not in the same category. Manners and affluence exclude them. Zacchaeus and I have been told we were sinners every day of our lives; we've been branded as such and shunned. People cross the street to avoid our shadows touching them lest they somehow become contaminated. Contrition may be a condition for Jesus' salvation."

"Speaking of which, what is salvation? He's the Savoir of Israel, is he not?"

"That's a part of the prophecies about him, yes," Matthew says, "and it comes up in his declarations now and then."

"And everyone but me seems to know what it means."

"They more often than not assume his salvation is political in nature and refers to a restoration of self-rule. As David saved us from the Philistines and others from the Assyrians and still others from the Babylonians and the Macedonians, the Christ will save us from the Romans. I oversimplify, but I think that's the idea. It's the idea friend Judas seems to buy into anyway."

"And I take it by your tone that you don't."

Matthew shakes his head. "I know no more than you do, Thomas. The more he talks about his kingdom or his father's kingdom, the less it seems to fit any prototype I've ever encountered. It at times seems as though it's not even of this world; and, if it is, it's more a vague brotherhood of believers rather than a specific place. Maybe a different plane of being completely. I honestly don't know."

"But would you not agree then that, when he speaks of salvation, it is in the context of that kingdom whatever and wherever it is?"

"For the time being, yes, that would be my best guess."

Raising of Lazarus

J UDAS AGAIN WALKS shoulder to shoulder with Thomas and Matthew. Jesus' singling out of yet another publican to host them for a meal has finally apparently not only legitimized Levi Matthew's inclusion in the ranks of the chosen but, for the Judean, has indeed elevated him several degrees in status. This pleases Thomas, immediately beside the two of them. In the procession only the Master himself and the four fishermen are ahead of them. All the other disciples and the women are just behind them, and the ever growing masses from Perea and Jericho are farther back.

"It's happening," Judas tells both men, as though he's somehow in on whatever *it* is.

"Something is," Matthew agrees goodheartedly.

"Word'll be out and they'll come streaming in from Galilee and maybe a handful from Samaria."

"You going to be all right with that? A whole handful of Samaritans?" asks Thomas.

"If you want a popular uprising, you take every living, breathing body you can get," Judas, missing or dismissing the sarcasm, answers him jauntily. More likely the former. He's not a good listener when he's excited, which is clearly the case now.

Presently all eyes in the immediate company of Jesus are focused on a man running toward them. Jesus holds up his hand to signal a halt. Thomas recognizes the messenger as someone from the household in Bethany where two sisters, Mary and Martha, live together with their brother Lazarus. All three are especially dear to Jesus. One can almost see the walls of Jerusalem from their home.

"Come quickly," calls out the courier. "Your friend Lazarus is gravely ill."

"The end of his sickness," Jesus says, as if he already knows of it, "is the glory of God, not the death of this man."

At this, assuming that all will be well with their friends in Bethany, the disciples heave sighs of relief. The messenger, also taking Jesus' remark to mean that Lazarus will soon be up and about, turns and, with long strides, runs back to Bethany to deliver the good news to the ailing man's sisters and friends gathered at his bedside.

Jesus' entourage leisurely continue on their way toward Zion. The Master, in no apparent hurry, with frequency gathers his company around him to tell them, often obliquely in language rife with metaphor and parables, yet more about his forthcoming kingdom. Thomas detects an almost eerie intensity in his voice now that did not seem to be there earlier.

"Now of all times," Iscariot wants to know, "why can he not just say what he has to say straight out? Why so opaque? Just get to the point in language everybody can understand. Why insist on our guessing all the time?"

"The man's telling us things about God, not a topic that lends to easy explanation you'll have to agree," Thomas tells him.

"So?"

"Our minds are too small to comprehend such utter vastness; straightforward language will never do the trick. What he does in his parables and metaphors is give us snippets, impressions. Fleeting, fuzzy glimpses of God."

"Frankly I'd settle for something we can sink our teeth into."

"Maybe there are things he wants us to figure out later rather than sooner."

"But now of all times we need something concrete."

Jesus no longer dwells on the themes of death and destruction that haunted his followers as they were taking their leave of Galilee months earlier. He is mellow now. The receptions he has received in Perea and just recently in Jericho seem to have buoyed him up. He is in better spirits than his disciples have seen him in a long time. There are still moments, however, when he does seem distracted and slightly downcast.

He speaks a lot of his kingdom these days but still in nonspecific terms. No timeline is given except the occasional suggestion that its finalization is already in progress, although he says nothing about the roles his disciples will play when at last it comes into being. He says more about who's on the outside than who's on the inside. Appetite for material wealth is one of the great delineators of who's where.

On one occasion while they are yet a ways from Bethany a man approaches Jesus. "Master," he says, "do me a favor? My brother grabbed up all our inheritance and is keeping it for himself. Will you please tell him he has to share it with me?"

"No one appointed me the arbitrator of your affairs—that's not why I'm here," replies Jesus, dismissing the request. Then, turning to his disciples, he goes on to say, "Take notice of this and be on your guard against anything that has any taint of greed or covetousness about it. Material possessions should have no place in your lives at all."

Thereupon he tells them this parable:

"It so happened, the story goes, that a very wealthy farmer's land produced bumper crop on top of bumper crop, so much so that he ran out of space to store his grain. 'What can I do?' he asked himself. 'Where will I put my harvest?'

"He thought and thought about this and then thought some more. Finally he said, 'I know! I'll pull down the old barns and build some new ones. Bigger barns and more of them. Then I'll have places not only for my grain but for all my many other things as well. That done, I shall say to my soul, "Soul, you have it made! Eat, drink, and live the good life! Your future's secure!"'

"But God said to him, 'You, my man, are a fool! For this very night your soul will be required of you. Whose then will be all these riches you've stored up?'

"Such is the lot," Jesus tells them emphatically, "of every man who accumulates material things for himself but is impoverished in the things of God. Materialism is nothing less than today's idolatry, for where your heart is there will be your treasure also."

Thomas notices that Judas Iscariot winces when he hears the Nazarene say this.

Their master's standards for inclusion are as high as they have ever been. What he told them in the early days when they went up the mountain still apparently maintains.

One day Peter asks of him quite innocently, "Master, if my brother does me wrong, how many times am I obliged to forgive him? Would seven times be about right?"

"No," Jesus answers, "not seven times, but rather seventy times seven."

They are within a day's easy journey of Bethany. Jesus is still setting a relaxed pace, often isolating himself from his disciples either to pray or simply to ponder what is ahead. Knowing he wants to be alone, his followers saunter on in groups of three and four and in some instances only two. Thomas and Levi Matthew increasingly find themselves bringing up the rear.

"We're on the cusp of something," says Thomas at one point, "and I honestly have no clear idea as to what it is."

"When I was a boy and didn't know something, I was content because I knew my father knew everything," Matthew tells him. "Even when I grew older and discovered my father didn't know either, I was still content because I knew the rabbi knew. Then when I realized he didn't know either, I took refuge in the fact that the theologians knew. Now I see they know less than anybody. I am, however, slowly beginning to think Jesus does."

"Yes, I agree. He if anybody."

"Oh, he does. More than the great Moses, more than all the prophets put together, he knows the ways and mind of God. Of that I am convinced."

"Probably so," says Thomas, "but all of a sudden he's struggling with something. Look at him up there, head bent, shoulders stooped, staggering along. It's like he's dragging a huge log on his back and it's about to crush him. Couple days ago in the best of spirits. Now look at him."

Soon the Master straightens himself and begins to pick up his pace. His head is up, his body erect, his face fixed on something in the distance ahead. Thomas looks hard to see what he is looking at but can make out nothing beyond the landscape that's been about them for the better part of the day. There's nothing suddenly suggestive of urgency in Jesus' gait; it's just a bit less lackadaisical. He jerks his head to tell his disciples to catch up with him.

"What is it?" asks Peter, hastening to his side.

"Our friend Lazarus has fallen asleep," Jesus replies. "I have to awaken him."

"Why not just let him sleep?" asks Peter.

"Lazarus is dead," Jesus answers matter-of-factly. "Let's go to him."

This strikes Thomas and, no doubt, the others, as especially strange. Neither Jesus' words nor his manner bear so much as a trace either of grief or great distress. It is almost as if he has known of Lazarus's death all along and for some secret reason has kept it to himself. Back when the messenger came to them from Bethany to report that Lazarus was mortally ill, he seemed to dismiss the idea out of hand. Did he not know then, wonders Thomas, how serious the man's illness was? And why is there not more evidence of anxiety now?

By the time they do get to Bethany, Lazarus, they discover, has already been in his tomb four days. Mourners are still at the home of Mary and Martha. As soon as Jesus and his train reach the house, out rushes Martha to meet them.

"If only you had been here," she says to Jesus, "my brother would not have died."

"He will rise again," Jesus tells her.

"Yes," she answers him, "at the resurrection on the last day."

"I am the resurrection and the life," he then says. "If a man believes in me, though he was dead, yet shall he live."

Mary then also comes out and says the same as her sister—that is, that if Jesus had been there Lazarus would still be alive. Tears roll down both women's cheeks, already lined and drawn with their much grieving. The other mourners, now gathered about, are also moaning and crying softly.

Jesus too begins to weep. Through his tears he asks to see his friend's grave. They lead the company to a small cave, the mouth of which has been covered by a boulder.

"Roll aside the stone," Jesus tells them.

Martha reminds him that Lazarus is four days dead and by now would be decaying, but Jesus presses them to do as he asks, and so the boulder is rolled aside. Jesus then raises his eyes to heaven and prays. When his prayer is finished, he turns his gaze to the mouth of the cave and shouts, "Lazarus, come forth!"

There is no possibility this time of the deceased's merely being asleep. The whole place has the smell of death about. There is a sound of someone or something's stirring around inside the crypt. Then they see Lazarus slowly crawling out of his tomb, his hands and feet still girded by the winding sheets, a cloth wrapped around his face. They unbind him and take him home. He is as hale and sound as any of them.

Levi Matthew and Thomas reflect on this miracle later that same afternoon.

"Why did he weep? Jesus I mean," Thomas wonders out loud. "He knew all along Lazarus was not to remain dead. In fact, he even told us as much."

"Then it couldn't have been out of grief."

"Anybody else, knowing what he knew, would probably have been smiling to himself or might even have snickered. I would have. The tears were really for nothing."

"Not to his sisters, not to others who wept."

"I mean his tears," Thomas explains. "He stood there and cried as though his heart was utterly broken. You saw him. Those were real tears sliding down the sides of his nose. Honest-to-goodness tears. Why? Why did he weep like that for a man with whom he would shortly be sitting at the dinner table?"

Matthew doesn't know. "Maybe out of empathy," he suggests, "simply because people he loved were sad."

Thomas ponders that. "Fits, doesn't it?" he says, thinking as he speaks. "He hurts when other people are hurting, whether their pain makes sense to anybody else or not. I think you're right."

They do not dwell on this anomaly for long, because they are interrupted by a patently ecstatic Judas Iscariot, hurrying over to them. "A stroke of genius!" he exclaims. "Timing could not have been more perfect! Why am I not surprised? Brilliant! Absolutely brilliant!"

"You approve?" says Matthew.

"His greatest miracle yet! And he performs it in the shadow of the Temple. And almost on the very eve of the Passover. Look there, you can see the Temple from here."

Thomas looks and, sure enough, the Temple. He can just barely see it.

"Oh yes," Iscariot goes on, "we've witnessed his raising of the dead before, but never anyone so incontrovertibly dead as our friend Lazarus, never anyone who's been dead four days, whose corpse has been looked upon by dozens upon dozens of friends and relatives. His resurrection was witnessed by the very people who laid him out, the men who wrapped his cold body and bore it to his tomb. There'll not be a soul in Jerusalem who will not have heard of this ten times over by tomorrow morning. It will be the buzz of the city."

"And panic in the ranks of the Sanhedrin," says Matthew. "I fear for him more now than ever."

"Not I! It'll, of course, be a matter of days now before he makes his move. And, when he does, tens of thousands of people will be at his back. From Galilee and Samaria and Perea, Jericho and Jerusalem too, from the four corners of the earth; wait and see, they will be there throwing garlands and branches in his path, wrenching the robes from their own backs and throwing them too. God willing, maybe there'll be an army of angels as well. Who knows? A triumph like none, not even the Romans, have ever seen."

The Judean soon leaves them to share his insights with others.

"To look at him, you'd never think he'd been in his grave for four whole days. As spry and at the peak of his life as I've ever seen hum.

Maybe more so. Lazarus I mean," says Levi Matthew. "Wouldn't you say so?"

"As hale as I've seen him," agrees Thomas.

"'I am the resurrection and the life,' Jesus said. Was that what he meant?"

"You mean what he just did for Lazarus?"

Matthew nods. "If so, was he telling us he can do the same thing for other people? For us perhaps? Was he making some kind of statement about the afterlife? He does buy into the afterlife. The Sadducees don't, but he does. Claims up and down it's inferred in the Scriptures. One's essential self lives on. The body returns to dust but the self lives on."

"What he said is consistent with that idea, I'd say, but doesn't exactly underscore it," Thomas tells him. "I'm loath to read too much into a single line. This could just be about friend Lazarus and no more. If it goes beyond that, I think he'll let us know."

"I for one will be listening."

The Triumphal Entry

JUDAS ISCARIOT TURNS out to be a prophet.

It is the day after the Sabbath, but no ordinary Sabbath this one. It has been the Sabbath leading up to the greatest holy days of them all, Passover week, in anticipation of which thousands of pilgrims from Dan to Beersheba have already shown up in the Holy City and a smattering of Abraham's progeny from adjacent Gentile lands as well. By week's end yet larger migrations will arrive. The thoroughfares of Jerusalem, already thick with people, will be reaching the point of total congestion in coming days.

By the time the city markets open on this particular morning, word of Lazarus's being raised from the dead has reached every quarter of the metropolis. Within the first hour after dawn the merchants and early shoppers have raced personally or dispatched messengers back to their homes and neighborhoods to rouse those still abed to apprise them of the startling news. Throughout the next few hours the various versions of the event are devoured instantly, like spilt grain by famished grackles, piquing listeners' appetites for more and yet more. Good citizens of Bethany who witnessed the spectacle firsthand and just happened to be in town on necessary errands are mobbed like royalty.

By mid-morning an emergency meeting of the Sanhedrin is hastily called into session at the Temple. The Pharisees and Chief Priests are in a state of near panic. Nicodemus will later tell the followers of Jesus that he too was at the height of excitement, though not for the same reasons. He still nursed the idea that Jesus might turn out to be the Christ and that he was about to declare himself as such.

"What shall we do?" a much frenzied Caiaphas asks of his fellows.

"Whether or not this Lazarus has been truly raised from the

dead, of course, cannot be ascertained at this time," intrudes Annas, Caiaphas' father-in-law and the other Chief Priest. "What we do know is that the gathering multitude out there believes he indeed has been. 'The Christ!' they're saying everywhere. 'The Christ has come!'"

"And by that they mean that Nazarene," Caiaphas makes sure they know.

"Perennial thorn in our collective flesh. All we hold sacred— this body, this place, the country itself—are in jeopardy. It is now expedient that a single person be destroyed rather than a whole nation. And this Lazarus too. The dead should not be walking among the living. It only confuses them."

And thus the Jewish Council begins to lay its plans to apprehend Jesus to kill him.

Later that day Jesus and his company, reinforced by crowds from Jericho and Bethany as well as Perea, their ranks swelling like floods at springtime as they advance, approach Jerusalem from the east. On the slopes of the Mount of Olives in Bethphage, Jesus calls his train to a stop. Clearly visible from their vantage point is the Holy City, in the foreground its walls with their eastward gates and beyond them pennants and clusters of smaller buildings that define the marketplace and further on, at the highest point within the city, like a lighthouse above a rocky shoal, the Temple itself.

Jesus stands in place for some time, gazing at this scene which has raised the pulses of so many pilgrims over the centuries, rendering them momentarily breathless with its grandeur and holiness. Then, all at once, the disciples nearest him see tears forming in the corners of his eyes, then beginning to roll down either cheek. He makes no effort to brush them away, but moans softly like a mother over her lost or dying child.

"Oh, Jerusalem, Jerusalem!" he sobs. "How often would I have gathered your children to my bosom as a hen gathers her brood under her wings, but you would not have it. You did not know the hour of your visitation."

He is inconsolable. For long he lingers there weeping before going on. There is no letup, no instant when sadness gives way to joy. It is, thinks Thomas, as though his own heart is being crushed. "This time," he tells Matthew, "I think it is grief."

"And so also do I."

But they do go on

At Jesus' instruction a young donkey is acquired, and when they are yet a distance from the east gate Jesus is mounted upon the little pack animal to take him into the city. Iscariot, euphoric since the raising of Lazarus, is suddenly scowling.

"A little donkey?" he says to Thomas and Matthew at his side. "Why not a magnificent white charger? That would better befit him."

"He picked a pack of donkeys, not white chargers, to follow him in the first place," replies Levi Matthew. "Why, then, not another one to bear him to his throne? The donkey fits perfectly."

Though unbroken, the beast, barely equal to its task, is docile and makes no attempt to throw his rider. Rather he raises his head high and trots lightly as though he has no burden at all.

As they advance on Jerusalem, one segment of the crowd moves on ahead of the Nazarene, another picks up the rear, all shouting their lungs out, saying, "Hosanna! Here he comes in the name of the Lord! The King of Israel!"

There is even a smattering of Pharisees in the throng. Alarmed by what is being trumpeted, they quickly zigzag through the tight ranks immediately surrounding Jesus and call out to him, "Tell them to stop yelling that."

"If they were to become silent," he answers, "the very stones would cry out."

In the meantime the crowds outside the city and the crowds within continue to swell. Men plowing their fields for planting halt their oxen and quickly unyoke them to rush and join the growing throng. Women at their dough troughs kneading bread and lads at play in the streets immediately abandon their activities to do likewise.

People from the surrounding countryside come also—from winding paths and roadways and thoroughfares; like water from tributaries tumbling down mountainsides to join a roaring river, they stream into the teeming horde now engulfing Jesus' entourage. Self-appointed heralds run on ahead to roust others out of their homes and places of business and trade to join the masses.

"The Christ is coming!" shout the young men, racing toward the gates. "The King is nigh!"

As they close on the gates, people from the city and those who have arrived there ahead of the crowd busy themselves with throwing straw and garlands and palm branches to pave the pathway Jesus is taking. One man tears off his cloak to place atop the palms; another immediately does the same, with many, many others quickly doing likewise. Shawls and coats and blankets are also strewn along the way.

"It's Jesus!" some are crying out.

"The promised one is coming in the name of the Lord!" cry others. "Hallelujah! Our new David! The King! God bless the King!"

An excitement the likes of which no one in the throng can remember takes hold, feeding on itself, mounting with each step the small pack animal takes. There is a sense of something magnificent in this process and something yet more magnificent immediately ahead. Jesus passes through the gates, followed closely by his disciples—the once-interred Lazarus, walking tall, trailing some distance behind them. The people press in upon them from both sides but leave a corridor of three or four cubits so the procession can move freely in the direction of the Temple. The people are still tossing palm branches and garments onto the pathway before them.

The cheers of the masses reach an earsplitting crescendo.

"Son of David! Son of David!" they call out. "Hallelujah for the Son of David! Hallelujah for his everlasting reign!"

And as the train nears the Temple, two Pharisees on a porch are looking out over the great multitude in the streets. "Why, the whole world is falling in behind him!" Thomas hears one exclaiming to the other.

"At the moment," says the other, "but who knows what a day might bring?"

Straight up to the Temple Jesus rides, the crowd forming a half circle around him. There is, however, no latter-day Samuel on the

Temple steps waiting to press down upon his brow a kingly crown, only the usual corps of moneychangers behind their usual tables with their pouches of Temple coins to exchange, at handsome profit to themselves, for the drachmas and denarii of those who come from afar. Beyond these are the dealers of sacrificial livestock who grow fat by routinely rejecting supplicants' choice lambs in order to sell them their own. For these this is no more than a day of business as usual.

Jesus dismounts and, alone ascending the steps, heads for these merchants. The people who have been milling about and the horde of new arrivals one by one freeze in place, clearly anxious and fearful of what his next move might be. They all know how these merchants, with tacit consent of the Temple rulers, cheat poor religious folk at every turn in the name of the Lord God.

The Master stands for a moment before the money tables and then, with a sudden movement, heaves the first one on to its side and then the second clear over. Coins roll down the Temple steps, but no one so much as makes a move to pick any up. Even the children thereabouts are motionless and still.

For an instant Jesus faces the people. His jaw is set, and the lines about his forehead and mouth are rigid. And his eyes—the people have never seen such expression, such fire in his eyes or anyone's.

He kicks open the gate to the sheep pen, at the same time grabbing up a whip and lashing out at the men behind the tables. He then breaks open the dove cages. Swinging almost wildly now, he again darts back at the moneychangers. "My house shall be called a house of prayer," he thunders at them, "but you have made it a den of robbers!"

They all scatter from him like fowl before a fox.

It is a startling thing for the crowd to witness. Some break into cheers.

"He has to be the Christ!" shouts one man near where Thomas and Levi Mathew are now standing. "Such daring, such fire! Have we ever seen the likes in any other man? Only he could do this! Only the Christ is man enough! A manlier man I've never seen!"

"Nor have I," says Thomas to no one in particular.

All around them people are astir. It's as though they absolutely must move, for they cannot stand still. Some are literally dancing in the street and in front of the Temple. They are delirious with excitement. Hoots and whistles continue to fill the air. Wide-eyed and smiling, they all seem suspended in a state of high exultation.

Winding Down

By SUNDOWN THE crowd has all but dissipated. The last thread of fuchsia blends with the gray of the western sky to close the curtain on this, the most dramatic of days the disciples have ever spent with Jesus. Some men still stand about the Temple area in groups of six or eight, as if trying to prolong the day's adventure, but these too soon break from their fellows to retreat toward their homes or wherever else they might be spending the night.

Jesus has been spirited away by Peter, James, and John to a secret location where he'll be safe from the Temple rulers. Back to Bethany maybe. Thomas does not know, nor Judas either. For the sole Judean in Jesus' train this has clearly been a day that did not turn out as he expected. He is profoundly disappointed, as crestfallen as his fellows have ever seen him.

"I don't get it," he says loudly to the Zealot. "He embraces the Romans' moneymen and goes after our own with a whip. They were just trying to make a living like anybody else, and he treats them like villains of the worst kind."

"They are villains of the worst kind. That's why the people cheered him on."

"He could have waited though. That's my point. Could have officially eased them out, if he so disapproved, when he took things over. Could have driven them out, whipped them raw tomorrow, the day after tomorrow, a week from now. You don't clean house till it's your house. Bad timing, if nothing else."

"It is his house. We all heard him call it that."

"That we did," snaps back Iscariot. "And so did the High Priests and the rest of the Sanhedrin. They already damn him as a blasphemer. This only reinforces that charge. They'll make it into anything that serves them. If they weren't after his blood before, they will be now. And he was so close to pulling if off! So close, Simon! Why didn't he clinch it when all he had to do was reach out and wrap his fingers around it?"

"I don't know. Could be waiting for the Passover."

"For three years now he's been working up to it, and today it was being handed to him. And what does he do? He backs off and in the process finds a way to alienate every man of position in the city who could have given him that extra push to bring it off. So close, and he comes up with a cipher!"

"He needs someone to give him a push? Come now."

"Yes. Today for the first time that thought did cross my mind," Iscariot tells him. "The Temple rulers will not stand idly by. Time is of the essence. Somebody has to get in there now to get it rolling."

For the next three days, though, the Sanhedrin does stand idly by— this in appearance only however. In their private conclaves they are ever plotting strategies whereby to assassinate Jesus outright or to arrest him and draw in the Romans for the kill. But they do fear the substantial crowds forever surrounding their prey. At the least hint of a scuffle a hundred men would rush to his rescue and twice or three times that number would certainly witness the spectacle. Caiaphas cannot risk that. When they take him, they will have to do so when he is alone or is guarded by only a handful of men. Daytime is out. And so also are evenings, for, just before the crowds begin to thin out each afternoon, Jesus' friends seem somehow able to whisk him away to places unknown.

The Temple rulers' strategy now, Nicodemus is quick to discover, is twofold.

One ploy is rumormongering: taking snippets from Jesus' statements out of context as proofs of insurrection or blasphemy, twisting what he says for the same effect, and outright lying. He refers to God as his father, thus putting himself on a plane with God. Blasphemy for certain! It little matters that he refers to God as everybody else's father also.

Jesus has also predicted that the Temple will be destroyed, with not one stone resting upon another, and that he will raise it up again in three days. Although this is not an image any true Israelite takes to kindly, at worst it's a prophecy that will or will not come to pass. Nicodemus thinks it's just a metaphor for some thing or another. But blasphemy again! cry the rumormongers. And sure evidence of insurrectionism too! And out they rush to tell people Jesus is planning to tear down the Temple.

The Sanhedrin's other ploy is to discredit Jesus by putting him on the defensive in public forums. They march en masse to wherever he is preaching. Charging through his audiences, they loudly demand to know by what right he takes it upon himself to chase the bankers and livestock dealers from the Temple steps, by what right he speaks so confidently of things unseen and unknown. And they construct dilemmas to impale him upon, but more often than not they themselves are the ones getting transfixed by one horn or the other.

"Tell us! Just tell us by whose authority you act and speak," they press. "Who gave you the right to do what you're doing and say what you're saying? Tell us!"

"All right, if you will first answer a question for me," Jesus says to them. "John the Baptizer's practice of baptism—tell me, did that come from God? Or was it a purely human ritual?"

The Pharisees step away to get their heads together. Nicodemus is close enough to make out what they are saying: *If we say from God, he'll ask why we didn't believe him. If we say of purely human invention, this mob here, convinced the Baptizer was a prophet, will start heaving stones at us. We'll be lucky to get out alive.*

"Sorry," admits their spokesman, as they face Jesus again, "we can't tell you the source of John's authority."

"In that case," says Jesus, "I can't tell you the source of mine either."

This is just the beginning. A short while later along comes another pack of Pharisees. "Tell us, master, should we pay taxes to Caesar or not?" one of their number asks Jesus.

It is no secret in Jerusalem that Caesar is a tyrant and, therefore, no Jew is ever going to stand for a rabbi who commands him to pay taxes to him. But, if Jesus says not to pay taxes, the city fathers will cite him as an insurrectionist to Pontius Pilate, the Tetrarch, in which event he will likely be arrested. They mean to have him either way.

"Come, come, what is this really about? Is it my pleasure to address a concerned citizen or possibly a conniving blackguard engaged in some kind of ecclesiastical roguery? Ah, is that it?" Jesus, raising his brows and looking the Pharisee straight in the face, asks the man. "All right, come on then. Show me a piece of your tax money."

Someone hands a Roman denarius to the Pharisee, who in turn gives it to Jesus.

Jesus scrutinizes the coin first on one side and then, flipping it, on the other. "There's an image stamped on this coin," he says, handing it back to the Pharisee for his examination. "See if you can make out whose image it is. Can you tell?"

"Caesar's," the man replies.

"Oh yes, and I notice there's a name inscribed on the other side of it," Jesus observes next. "Whose name might that possibly be."

Again the man says, "Caesar's."

"Very good!" Jesus says. "Would it not be proper then to give to Caesar what belongs to him and, conversely, give to God what is His?"

Before long a covey of Sadducees advances upon the crowd from a different direction and slowly begins to infiltrate it, the men breaking ranks and working their ways individually to the front. These are leading citizens who hold in ridicule the idea of life after death because the Scriptures only by inference suggest it and do not address it outrightly. Their sanctimonious demeanors and fine robes set them off from the rest of the people. However, they are almost comic in that they are trying so hard to appear as no more than regular, run-of-the-mill spectators. Finally stationing themselves directly in front of Jesus, one of them lifts his hand to signal he has a question.

Jesus nods politely to him. "Yes," he says.

"I have a problem with something, master," the man tells him. "Maybe you can help me work it out. If I correctly recall, Moses commanded that, if a married man dies without children, his brother should take to wife his widow and raise up a family for him. I am right on that, am I not?"

Again Jesus nods. "Go on."

"Okay, I heard of an instance of a man's dying and leaving no issue. Dutifully the oldest of his six brothers marries this man's widow. Unfortunately for himself and her he also soon dies leaving her still childless. The next brother in line, heedful of Moses, then marries her, but he too dies without issue. And that's not the end. His next brother dies as well. And so it is that, honoring Moses, all six of the original husband's brothers in succession eventually wind up marrying the same woman. A very fatally flawed line of brothers, you'd have to say."

"Not only very fatally flawed, but more than likely very fictional as well."

"Be that as it may, let me get to my question. In time the woman herself dies. Now, since she has married all seven brothers, at the resurrection of the dead whose wife will she be? It's a problem, you'll have to admit, exponentially larger than that resolved by Solomon over who gets the baby." The Sadducee does not even try to hide his smirk as he says this.

"Marrying and the begetting of children are features of people's temporal existence," Jesus tells him. "The whole idea of family in the eternal realm is entirely different. If you thought about it, you would see that it has to be. Death simply does not exist there. God himself is the great father of all. Temporal relationships are virtually dissolved by the fact that everyone who enters into His presence is, first and foremost, His own son or daughter. Now, let me ask you a question. Is God the God of the living or the God of the dead?"

"The God of the living most certainly," answers the Sadducee. "Why do you ask?"

"You speak so glibly of Moses and yet seem to forget the story of his burning bush encounter with God. You surely must remember that God on that occasion said, 'I am the God of Abraham, Isaac, and Jacob.' This is roughly four to five hundred years after these men died, is that not true?"

The man does not answer.

"So you agree? If God is, as you also agree, the God of the living, does this not mean that these forebears of ours, these people of faith, must have been living at the time God spoke to Moses out of the burning bush? He said, 'I *am* the God of Abraham, Isaac, and Jacob.' I think we can conclude then, can we not, that all people, although maybe no longer in temporal existence, are alive to God?"

This exchange with the Sadducees is sharp and on target. Nicodemus regrets that none of his fellow Pharisees are there to hear it. For some reason it brings to his mind a comment Jesus made when he was wrangling with some theologians right there at the Temple on his previous visit. "Before Abraham even existed, I am," he said on that occasion. It struck the young Pharisee at the time as strange, but those were his exact words. *How could that be?* he wondered then and now does again.

Shortly after this they are outside the Temple. Jesus stands there studying the people going up to the treasury boxes to give their tithes and offerings. Most of the donors are well attired and strut confidently forward to deposit their gifts, conspicuously dropping fistfuls of silver shekels into the boxes and then marching, heads high, back through the crowd.

At one point, however, an old woman steps forward. She is wearing widow's weeds, threadbare rags to be more exact, and moves cautiously toward the boxes. Hesitating but for a moment before a box, she reaches out to drop but two copper mites into it. There is no discernible sound as the coppers hit the mound of silver already there. She hangs her head, almost as though in shame, as she walks away.

Jesus quietly calls attention to this. "Did you see that?" he asks his audience. "This poor widow has given more than all these others. They have tossed nothing more than their spare change into the coffers, whereas she has given her whole livelihood."

And so the days pass, three of them, and nothing happens. There are no healings, no miracles of any kind; other than a dwindling number of verbal conflicts, all of which are resolved in Jesus' favor, there are no clashes either of raised swords or raised voices. There's a calm.

But that's not to say nothing's going on behind the scenes, for there is. A great deal.

The disciples do not know until much later that Judas Iscariot is involved in secret talks with Caiaphas and Annas—at night, of course, when he will not be missed and nor be seen going to the Temple. Whether his purpose is to give up on Jesus or to force him into some action they will never know. The Judean puts on a good act around them, saying the things he's always said, showing the moods he's always shown, aping the responses of the others when Jesus says or does something.

Nevertheless they all sense that there's something in the wind. Something is about to happen. When by day's end on the third day all the Pharisees and theologians abruptly stop badgering the Nazarene and then seem to vanish, the disciples know almost for certain something is imminent. In the depth of their souls they feel it. A fear like none they've ever known begins to sweep over them. They stay more tightly grouped together. Peter begins to wear a short sword under his robe again. A cloud of deep dread envelops them.

The Night Before

NOT ONLY HAVE Thomas and Matthew never spoken with the man they are now supposed to find and follow; neither to their knowledge has ever even seen him. But there he is, walking away from the marketplace, just as Jesus predicted, carrying a jug of water. The two spot him at the same instant and, neither saying a word, begin to trail after him, staying a dozen or so paces behind him,. Presently he stops in front of a sizable house and, unlatching the door, commences to enter it.

The two disciples pick up their paces. "Good sir," calls out Thomas.

Now at the threshold, the man turns to them. "Yes?"

"The Master sent us," Matthew tells him. "He wants to know in which room he and his disciples are supposed to celebrate the Passover. We do have the right house, do we not?"

The householder evidences no surprise. It's as though he has been expecting them. "Do come in," he invites them and, once they are inside, takes them up a set of stairs to a large room that occupies the whole second floor. There's an ample oblong table in the center of the room and, placed strategically about the room, by quick count, exactly thirteen chairs. "There will be cups, plates, knives if you need them, he tells them, "and serving dishes along with, of course, a basin for water and a towel,"

Astonished by how such detailed arrangements could be effected without their knowing, the two disciples take their leave and return to the street.

"It reminds me of his sending us out to get that unbroken donkey he rode into Jerusalem on," says Thomas.

"I was thinking the same."

"Where do these mystery people come from? That they would oblige him is not remarkable, but that he would know them is. We've certainly never seen them before. You wonder if he has."

"I can't see how."

And so it is that, shortly before dusk that evening, the two disciples, bringing with them, as instructed, sufficient bread, wine, and other essentials for the meal, join their companions in this upstairs room. The owner is nowhere to be seen but, as promised, has arranged the chairs around the table and set out the necessaries for their Passover supper. Thomas takes note that one chair is out a ways from the table and slightly askew. On it is a towel. A basin sits next to it and beside the basin the ewer of water they'd seen the householder carrying from the marketplace earlier in the day.

Jesus, upon their entering, chooses the odd chair for himself. He takes off his cloak and drapes it across the back. And then, taking off his outer clothes and placing them over his cloak, he carefully pours the water from the ewer into the basin. Having done this, he wraps the towel around his waist. Then, motioning one of the disciples to be seated, he kneels down and commences to wash the man's feet, drying them with the towel. After him, he repeats the process with another disciple and then another.

When Simon Peter's turn comes, he momentarily balks. "Lord, are you going to wash my feet?"

"I realize, dear Peter, you do not understand what I'm doing, but you will."

"No, I cannot let you wash my feet!"

"If I do not wash you, you can have no part of me."

"In that case, please do, but not just my feet. Wash my hands and face as well!"

Thomas scrutinizes the scene as Peter takes the chair. Jesus gazes up at him more intensely than he has ever looked at any of them before. His eyes are heavy with not the least hint of the customary sparkle in them whatsoever.

"If a man's clean to begin with, dear Peter, the feet are enough," he tells him. "He's clean throughout." Then, having washed and dried both of the disciple's feet, he says, "There, I pronounce you clean, which is not exactly true of everyone in this room. I say this now because something is about to happen that I want you to know about before it does. Thus will you be able to believe I am indeed the person I claim to be."

Up until now dinners with Jesus have been festive occasions, Jesus himself good-naturedly providing the preponderance of wit and lively conversation. But not so now. This night finds him pensive and preoccupied. His movements, his eyes, his brow, his soft voice all bespeak a troubled and somber spirit. Thomas sees his pain. With all his heart he yearns to say or do something to lessen it but can think of nothing that would achieve that end. The other disciples around the table seem to be picking up on this too. Something is afoot that Jesus knows and they do not. A subtle fear, like an evening fog, begins to permeate the upstairs chamber.

"Oh, my children, try not to be anxious," Jesus, soon rising from his chair, tells them. "It is so important that I eat this meal with you! Our time is very short. This is the last such meal we'll be eating together—for the time being anyway. The hour is fast upon us when I will be going where you cannot follow. The wheels are already in motion."

"But I will follow you!" blurts out Peter.

"You will follow me?"

"Yes," insists the onetime fisherman, "into the very jaws of death!"

"You will lay down your life for me?"

"Yes!" he says louder, more emphatically.

"Oh, Peter, my dear Peter," Jesus tells him. "Before the cock crows twice tomorrow morning you will have disowned me three times. You'll tell men you never even knew me."

To this the big man has no response. He seems completely befuddled by Jesus' words. Jesus pauses before going on, then says, looking at each disciple in turn, "When I'm gone, there's something I want you to do for me, which is simply to love one another. This will be the only way people out there will know for certain that you're my disciples. Will you do that for me?"

The men indicate by nods and uplifted eyebrows that they will.

"All right then, let's eat in earnest," Jesus says to them, picking up one of the loaves of bread and raising his head heavenward to offer up a prayer of thanks. His prayer ended, he breaks the loaf in two and then into smaller pieces. "Whenever you get together like this to eat," he says, as he quietly passes the morsels around to his disciples, "remember me when you do it. Try to think of this bread as my body, which is broken for you. Let it be a reminder to you of that fact. Go ahead now and eat it."

This they commence to do—albeit, in view of the image he has just evoked, somewhat apprehensively. Thomas suddenly finds himself not nearly as hungry as he thought he was when they entered the upper room a short time earlier. He cannot, as he slowly chews and then tries to swallow the food in his mouth, fail to dwell upon the symbolic import Jesus assigned the bread. It does not go down easily.

Later, when they have eaten, Jesus lifts up the wine chalice.

"And try to think of the wine in this cup as my blood which is shed for many. I do have to tell you, though, that there is one person at this table who will shortly betray me. This will be my last wine before I drink it afresh in the Kingdom of God."

Having said this, he offers up another prayer of thanks and then passes the chalice to his disciples so each can drink in turn. Again the image Jesus has called up is so unsettling that the wine sits in Thomas's mouth for some time before he is able to swallow it.

They eat on in silence, each man somber and, like Thomas, no doubt turning over and over in his mind the macabre significance of the bread and the wine, at the same time deeply troubled by Jesus' almost parenthetical comment that someone in their midst is about to betray him. Thomas can neither grasp exactly what he means by "betray" nor imagine who in their ranks is capable of such treachery. Each man furtively looks slowly to his right and then his left for some clue as to who the wretch might be. John is seated next to Jesus. Peter calls over to him, "Who's he talking about?"

John in place turns to Jesus. "And who is this, Lord?"

"It isn't me, Lord, is it?" asks Nathanael.

Jesus assures him it is not. Then six or eight other disciples ask the same question of Jesus, and to each he shakes his head and says no. "It's the man I'm giving this bread to after I've dipped it," he finally tells them. He thereupon breaks off a piece of bread from a loaf and dips it in his wine and beckons Judas Iscariot to come to him.

Giving Judas the bread, in a hushed voice he says to him, "I understand you have business to attend to. Do be quick about it."

Judas leaves forthwith.

Thomas assumes, as probably do the others, that since Judas is bursar to the group Jesus is sending him out to buy more food or maybe something else he suddenly realizes they might need. No one at the time makes any connection between what Jesus has just said and his excusing Iscariot from their company.

"Do not become overly anxious about all this," Jesus next tells them. "You must not let your faith in God or in me falter. In my Father's estate there are many mansions. I will go on ahead and get everything ready for you, and then I'll come back and escort you there myself. Now you know where I'm going as well as the pathway to get there."

Thomas does not know where he is going and says as much. "I don't get it, Lord," he says. "I honestly don't know where you're going. So how can I know the way to get there?"

"I myself am the way!" Jesus responds. "I am all you need—the truth, the life, everything—the only pathway there is to the Father. No man comes to him except through me."

"Why don't you show us God then?" asks Philip.

"Have I been with you so long, Philip, and you still don't know me? If you've seen me, you've already seen Him. How can you say, 'Show us God'? I am in Him, and He's in me!"

Jesus goes on talking in this vein, at moments, like a father himself trying to reassure his children that all will be well and at other moments somberly underscoring the fact that something enormously troubling is imminent. Remembering earlier comments about his impending death, Thomas concludes that he is trying to prepare them for that grim eventuality.

Others wonder out loud if perhaps he's anticipating a solo trip into some distant land, which he assumes they know about—but, not having picked up on his cues, they do not. He also talks about his kingdom and his ties to God, although his words seem to fall on rocky ground. When he finally finishes his discourse, they sing a psalm together and then exit the room to go out into the night. There's a chill in the outside air and it's very dark.

Jesus, flanked by Peter and the brothers Bar-Zebedee, goes off in the direction of the Mount of Olives to a secluded garden just beyond the Kidron valley where he often retreated to pray. The other disciples, in twos and threes, head for the homes where they are staying. And Judas is nowhere to be seen; his errand, whatever it was, is taking him longer than expected. For the second evening in a row, although bone tired, none of the men are looking forward to a good night's sleep.

Thomas is with Matthew. They walk on in silence, both troubled to the quick by Jesus' none too ambiguous statement that they have eaten their very last meal together, and neither is especially anxious to explore the limited explanations as to what exactly he might have meant by it. In tone and phrasing there was nothing to suggest he was predicting his imminent coronation. Thus when Thomas mumbles, more to himself than his companion, that there is something awful afoot, he speaks with clarity for both.

"And we don't know what to do," Matthew responds.

"He talks of death and mansions almost in the same breath."

"Twice now we have seen him weep—almost uncontrollably. Heavy seems his heart, about to break you'd think."

"Already broken more than likely."

"What went wrong? What's going wrong? Is the problem somehow with us? Have we failed him in some way? He's given us no instructions, just to remember him whenever we get together to break bread. That tells us nothing."

"Except that, when we do, he's no longer going to be there."

"None of it fits with everything he's said about his kingdom over the past three years. What happened to that, don't you wonder? He talked so much about it—the great kingdom of God on earth. Defined who would be in it and who wouldn't, an ethic of states of mind and values as well as words and action; a domain where piety for public consumption has no place and simple loving kindness is the rule of the land. Was that but a dream we'll simply dream no more?"

"He has power over storms at sea, over every disease imaginable, over death. Power in his voice, in his touch, his fingertips. His magic extends to feeding multitudes. Can it not extend to laying low the mighty as well?"

"Has it suddenly vanished, do you think? Has he for some reason surrendered it? Woof! It's gone, disappeared? What's happened? And what's going to happen?"

And so the two continue toward their destination, to their lodging where they know they will neither be able to sleep nor happen upon a single answer to the hundreds of questions that race through their minds. Along the way both catch themselves asking the same things they'd asked earlier and, out of weariness and a sense of futility, elect to finish their journey in silence.

At their quarters the two men are soon twisting and turning on their respective pallets, eyes wide open, peering into the darkness as though for a distant spark of light that does not appear, not the least flicker anywhere at all. Clouds have now covered the heavens to close out the moon and stars.

"Will his kingdom ever, ever come?" Thomas asks.

"I don't know. I used to know things, but I don't anymore."

"If it doesn't, why then did he come?"

"I fear for him, Thomas."

"And I too."

The Trials

NEITHER MAN HAS slept a wink by the time, hours later, Simon the Zealot, torch in hand, bursts into their room to announce that Jesus has been taken by the Temple guards and is at that very moment being hauled off to Annas's courtyard to be tried. Thomas and Matthew are up in an instant to join their young comrade in rousting the others.

"Was in the Garden of Gethsemane at prayer when they ambushed him," the onetime insurrectionist tells them. "Peter and the Zebedee brothers were there but caught off guard. It seems the big man took a swipe at one of them, but Jesus told him to put away his sword. Then they were off with him."

"No struggle?" asks Levi Matthew.

"Apparently none."

"Time was when he could have walked straight through the middle of them without breaking a sweat. We've seen him do it. Could have parted them like the Red Sea."

"No resistance at all. Almost like he was expecting them."

"Gethsemane was his secret place," says Thomas. "How did they know to find him there?"

"Judas. Apparently Judas Iscariot told them. Led them right to the spot and then pointed Jesus out to them by kissing him. Frustrated man that one."

"And damned too."

The three men by torchlight make their ways as speedily as possible into the city, detouring only to fetch Nathanael and Philip and the other James en route. Though heavy clouds stretch out over the eastern horizon, there is a hint of approaching dawn as they approach the Temple area and the palatial quarters of Annas, titular

High Priest and father-in-law to the de facto High Priest Caiaphas. The courtyard is already crowded, primarily with parties hostile to Jesus. The disciples manage, however, to squeeze singly into the still empty spaces here and there.

It becomes quickly apparent to Thomas that, in the rough ways the Sanhedrin's rogues are treating Jesus and the chorus of charges they are announcing against him, the trial taking place is nothing but sham, no more than theatrical justice for the consumption of the gathering masses which now already extend into a semicircle more than twenty cubits deep in Annas's courtyard. He knifes his way through the crowd to where Levi Matthew is standing.

"He's totally innocent," he tells his companion. "What are they doing?"

"Trying to make people think he's getting a fair hearing."

"He isn't, and they have to know that."

It is just then that Simon the Zealot slips in beside the two. "The fact there's a trial at all is what matters," he contributes. "They only need the illusion of due process, so they can tell the people he had his day in court, that the procedure was right and proper."

"What people?"

"The Romans chiefly. 'We had a trial and found him guilty' is what they'll be telling Pilate."

"Guilty of what?"

"Whatever they say he's guilty of. Sacrilege, violations of two or three Commandments, a plot to raze the Temple, insurrection, rioting—whatever suits them. Trust them to be specific. Just plain, bare-bones guilty won't do."

"That isn't a trial."

"No, it isn't," comes another voice behind them. They turn to see Nicodemus, the young Pharisee they have been used to seeing at the edges of the Jesus' crowds each day since their return to Jerusalem. "It's a ritual to convince the people that the charges, if not valid, are reasonable. As long as he is proved guilty of something and the process itself passes muster and the hordes do not take to the streets, his accusers will have enough to enlist the Romans."

"You're serious."

"I would that I weren't," says Nicodemus. "A semblance of a trial is all they need in order to drag him off to the Roman governor. Before him it'll be an entirely different list of charges—not blasphemy and disregard for the Laws of Moses but insurrection against their overlords themselves. It's been the Sanhedrin's strategy from the start. I didn't know it had reached this stage."

"They'll try him again before the Romans?"

"Before Pontius Pilate, the governor. It's always best if the Romans are fully responsible for the disposing of malcontents or at very least complicit in the council's shenanigans. Herod, governor of Galilee, obliged them in ridding them of the Baptizer. Pilate needs to be cajoled into lending assistance this time."

"But does he does not know who he is?" asks Simon as if in astonishment.

"Only as a threat to his own authority."

"He's the Christ! He has power over life and death! He can raise up cripples and give sight to the blind! He can quiet a raging, torrential storm with but a word! Has the power of God himself in his fingertips! Do they not know whom they're taking on? How dare they?"

"So far he has not raised a whisper against them."

"When he does, let them beware! He'll rain down the full fury of heaven upon them!"

"If he wants to," inserts Matthew. "We have no indication yet that he does."

"He won't abide them forever."

"He might. We don't know."

"But what about his kingdom?"

"We don't really know about the when and where of that either, do we? Or even its nature?"

While they talk, the trial of Jesus formally begins. Order is called for by Annas and Caiaphas, and witnesses, one after another, come forward.

"Invokes the powers of darkness in his black magic," says one.

And the witness after him claims much the same, saying he saw him doing so with his own eyes.

"Tells everybody he's going to tear down the Temple so there's not one stone standing upon another. Then he's going to build it again in three days," yet another man testifies.

This is confirmed by the next.

"Calls the Lord God Jehovah his very own father," asserts the one after him.

"His mouth's full of blasphemies," says yet another.

And so on and so on.

They use phrases and snippets from actual statements, but out of context, to smear Jesus and represent him as saying just the opposite of what he really did. And then come the boldfaced lies, lies as transparent as isinglass, perjuries as glaring as the sun itself now beginning to peek above the eastern horizon.

But Jesus stands there without so much as lifting an eyebrow against his accusers. He lets them beat, mock, and spit at him. Anyone familiar with the great Galilean, Thomas knows, can refute them. For Jesus himself it should be child's play. But he stands there, himself silent. Thomas does not understand; not one whit does he understand.

"Tell them! Tell them!" cries out the Zealot by his side. "Remember that Sabbath at the synagogue? Remember that morning in front of the Temple? Remember their questions on taxes, on the resurrection? You told them then. Tell them now! Oh, please tell them now!"

But Jesus does not.

Thomas looks about him, and off to the side near a fire he sees Peter, Jesus' Rock, yelling something to a girl, also by the fire, but he is too far away and the ruckus between them too thunderous to hear what he is saying. Elsewhere he spots Nathanael and Philip. They too look aghast at the spectacle taking place before them but say nothing. Only Simon, the youngest of the disciples and the only one Thomas knows who might have blood on his hands, is shaking his fists in the air and shouting out in protest. Judas Iscariot is nowhere to be seen.

Thomas is aghast. *What's come over us? Why so tongueless all of a sudden? Why so frightened to death? Why so void of speech and spine? Of all the rogues that walk this earth, why are we so utterly without heart and soul?*

He stands frozen by shame, as unable to move as to speak, as unable to comprehend as to think. None of this makes sense to him. His thoughts seem to spin, unconnected, in his head, absent of both substance and congruity. Is he mad? Has something snapped, some part of him been crushed, something unmanned him? Yesterday he was beginning to know the way, the truth, and the life; today he knows nothing again, this time with a profound and piercing sense of loss.

Compounding his impotence, and quite possibly contributing to it, is Jesus' own refusal to do no more than just stand there as they disparage and brutalize him. He denies nothing, makes no attempt at all to call his accusers on the most blatant of their perjured testimony, endures their physical abuse without lifting his arms to ward off blows. When they strike him on the right side, he turns so they can batter him on his left as well. He is like a lamb set upon by dogs in confined quarters; like one of the hopeless, helpless street beggars he himself was wont to single out and heal.

Act! Do something! Put an end to this charade!

The one they still sometimes call the Twin glances about him to find that Simon the Zealot has suddenly moved on. So also have Levi Matthew and the young Pharisee Nicodemus. Everybody seems to be in motion, retreating from the courtyard of Annas; some leaving the scene apparently to return to their homes or places of employment, others to the alleyways and streets leading to the Roman quarter of the city. Almost automatically, without consciously intending to do so, Thomas follows. This trial is apparently over, a new one about to commence.

Simon's prediction of fury raining down from heaven proves baseless. Daylight is full upon them now, and there has been no disruption in the heavens at all, no earthshaking bolts of thunder, no squadron of angelic beings sweeping down upon them. Leaderless except for their manipulators and their dogs, the rabble's herd instinct drives on toward the palatial abode of Pontius Pilate. In front are the

Sanhedrin dignitaries themselves, Annas and Caiaphas, a step but no more, ahead of the rest; then the guards making sure their prey keeps pace, who, though battered and downcast, obliges them by doing so; then the masses, now predominately made up of the Galilean's detractors—his champions having left the scene for duties elsewhere or, more likely, Thomas surmises, out of fear that they too might be caught up in the sweep.

The horror of what is ahead stabs at Thomas's heart. He is resolved now, however, to see it through to the end. Pilate will not be an easy sell—that much he knows—and that fact may be the only palpable hope there is now. The Roman does not want to takes sides in the petty religious squabbles of his subjects. Keeping order and making sure the taxes continue to roll into the imperial treasury is what the tetrarchs are there for; anything else is for their Jewish leaders to take care of. Pilate could possibly balk.

And he does.

The Roman governor seems none too pleased about being rousted from his bed at this hour in the morning. He is gruff in voice and demeanor. Definitely not in a mood to be cajoled. Neither the Chief Priests nor their fellows miss this and so pull up short, ordering their heavies to advance their prisoner a dozen cubits or so closer to the porch where Pilate, not in receiving clothes, is standing.

"What's this?" he demands of the Temple rulers. "Do you have charges to make against this man?"

"Were he not a criminal, would we have brought him to you?" Caiaphas shouts back.

"Judge him then. You have laws."

"But we aren't permitted to put a man to death."

Technically this is true, Thomas knows. They're not allowed to put criminals to death, but he is sure of one thing: If this were a woman surprised in adultery or some poor peasant they'd caught yoking his ox on the Sabbath, they'd have already smashed in his skull and buried him under a ton of rocks. Oh no, it isn't out of respect for law, either theirs or his, that brings them to Pilate. The Tetrarch has to know that. Too many people love this villain of theirs.

"He's been corrupting the people," calls out his accuser. "Yes, he told them it was wrong for them to pay taxes to Caesar. Said he was king."

Obviously to placate them Pilate has Jesus brought into the villa so he can examine the man himself. The throng outside waits some time for the accused insurrectionist and governor to reappear, a rumble going through their ranks all the while, increasing in intensity the longer they have to wait. Their screaming reaches a peak so loud that Thomas thinks it might wake Rome's man in Egypt and all the dead in between. Trial by cacophony, a new wrinkle.

Pilate has to shout when he reappears on the porch with Jesus. It takes minutes before the crowd quiets down. "I find no fault in this man," he calls out. "He is not a criminal!"

Pandemonium breaks out. Whipped up by the priests and Pharisees—some probably paid by them as well, thinks Thomas—the protesters all start to shout back at once. Their faces are livid with rage. One would think Pilate had poisoned their Passover wine or run a herd of pigs through the Temple.

"He's an agitator!" some cry out.

"Been stirring up the people everywhere—all the way between here and Galilee."

"He's setting himself up as a king. Caesar's enemy. Tells the people not to pay taxes. Conspires to tear down Herod's Temple."

Suddenly Pontius Pilate seems to see his out. He obviously has no stomach to kill this man, but that is what they are asking, thunderously demanding. For some reason they need him, the Roman governor, to take the fall, and he does not want to do so. And in an instant now, as though struck by a bolt from out of the blue, his dodge is handed him. Holding up his arms to still the crowd, he pulls himself up to his full height, a hint of relief on his face.

"You say he's been in Galilee," he says to Caiaphas. "Does that mean he's a Galilean?"

"Yes, a Galilean," the Chief Priest affirms.

"That settles it," then says Pilate. "Herod, his own governor, is in the city right now. Let him judge him."

And with that, the Tetrarch turns and retreats into his villa.

Jesus' judges stand momentarily agog.

Soon, with Caiaphas directing the armed men surrounding the Nazarene away from Pilate's villa, the procession heads back into the city proper in the direction of King Herod's lush Jerusalem quarters. From a ways back Thomas follows them, and from yet farther back, in single file, silently, dejectedly, so also do ten of Jesus' other disciples. Levi Matthew drops back so that he and Thomas are together bringing up the rear. Huddled over, stoop-shouldered, like a long-toothed draft animals pulling a plow, they trudge on. A great heaviness weighs upon them.

Neither man now expects any good will come from an audience with King Herod. If Herodias and Salome, the blood of one prophet already on their hands, prove to have accompanied the Galilean governor to the Holy City, who knows what will happen?

Thomas is now physically ill. By force of will alone he lifts his feet to stay in step with the others. "I'm sticking with him to the bitter end, Matthew," he tells his friend, "which could well turn out to be the case."

Matthew grimly agrees. "Pilate was his last best chance. But that too seems to have evaporated. He surely had to know Jesus isn't an insurgent and could have ordered his immediate release."

"Or, at the very least, have declined to be complicit in the Sanhedrin's little murder plot."

"If Jesus' blood were to be totally on the Jewish hierarchy's hands, they might possibly have relented, because at heart they're scared stiff of popular reaction."

"But Pilate, the political animal that he is, defers—sends them all off to Herod and goes in to wash his hands of the whole business. A little shuffle back and forth, no more."

"And Herod will at last meet his own province's most celebrated citizen, but, once he sees he's being handed a viper, he'll throw it back at them and run helter-skelter for the comfort of Herodias's bosom."

"And Jesus'll be right back in Pilate's court within the hour."

And so he is.

Child that he is, Herod is thrilled with his unexpected guest and in his inimitably tactless way invites him to perform a little magic for his personal amusement. When Jesus doesn't oblige him, he quickly loses interest in him altogether and hands him over to his hangers-on to play their own games with the Nazarene. They, in turn, blindfold him and take turns punching and slapping him about and asking him to guess which one delivers each blow. But Herod quickly tires of this as well and, as his part of what he takes to be little more than a practical joke, decks Jesus in one of his castoff robes and sends him promptly back to his friend Pilate. All, as predicted, within the hour.

Pilate in the meantime has breakfasted and changed into his most official-looking tunic and is back out on his porch again when the mob, angrier than ever, returns to his villa. The Roman governor has had time to think and has apparently come up with a ploy that, by the way he carries himself, he seems personally quite pleased with.

"Hear me, men of Jerusalem," he calls out to them. "It is, as you know, my custom ever since coming to Judea to release a prisoner to you at your Passover time. My gift for your holy day. I now have in my dungeon the single greatest villain to reside there in many a year. Barabbas. You all know Barabbas. And you also know that I find nothing criminal in this Jesus—no, nor does Herod either. We have heard your charges and find in him nothing worthy of death. As is my custom, this year I will release upon you either this man or Barabbas. You choose. Will it be this one here?"

"Not this man," they shout back. "Give us Barabbas!"

It is obvious to Thomas that the Sanhedrin is one step ahead of Pilate. Anticipating this ploy, they have to have put the crowd up to this. It's too spirited, too synchronized to be otherwise. Pilate has clearly miscalculated both how much the Jewish leaders understand him and how deeply they hate the Galilean.

His smirk disappears instantly. "What then would you have me do with this Jesus, who is called the Christ?" he asks.

"Let him be crucified!" with one voice they all shout.

In a clumsy maneuver to appease them short of bowing to this demand, Pilate orders his soldiers to haul Jesus off and flog him. This they do most zealously. Even from a distance Thomas can hear the thongs crack across Jesus' back. He studies the faces of the Temple rulers, which evince neither shame nor satisfaction.

On their own the soldiers, after they have flogged Jesus, take a cue from Herod and fashion a crown for him out of twisted twigs of thorns and press it down upon his head so that he begins to bleed along his brow and temples. They then drape him again in Herod's robe and genuflect in mock obeisance before him, shouting derisively, "Hail, King of the Jews!" And then they slap him with their open hands.

He is a frazzled and bloodstreaked sight when they parade him back to Pilate's porch, but, though visibly weakened, he is still able to walk on his own. With the crown of thorns on his head and the kingly robe across his shoulders, his figure is one that should evoke pity rather than anger. Nothing about him is threatening in the least.

"Behold him!" Pilate now cries out mockingly, trying to underscore how thoroughly harmless he considers Jesus to be. "Behold the man!"

His sarcasm, however, in no way diminishes the Sanhedrin's fury. At the very sight of him, the Chief Priests and Pharisees scream out louder than ever, "Crucify him! Crucify him!"

Crucifixion

JESUS EMERGES FROM the Roman encampment bearing a thick-beamed cross on his back, the base of which drags on the uneven ground behind him. He is doubled over at the waist like someone pulling an oxcart; his head, also bent, is downcast. At first he staggers under the weight; then, bending his body yet further, he is able to correct his balance and move on. The base sporadically rises and dips when hitting the innumerable slits and gullies carved across the trail and then bumps almost rhythmically once they get to the paving stones.

From his vantage point atop a crest overlooking the pathway Thomas can see the lines of Roman soldiers on either side, with others ahead and behind keeping the spectators at bay. Although individuals in his escort shoot quick glances at him when he falters, none of them intervenes to help the Galilean carry his cross.

At one point, when they have gone a little less than a furlong, one of the soldiers bolts through the ranks of the onlookers and seizes a tall, muscular young man who is not part of the crowd at all but just happens to be in its vicinity. In skin tone and profile the fellow does not seem to be native to that region at all. His garb and the way he carries himself mark the man more as a field hand or artisan than anything else, Thomas speculates, though he could simply be a Passover pilgrim—they come in a variety of shades these days. The soldier leads the man quickly by the wrist back through the spectators to where Jesus is dragging his cross.

"Give him a hand," barks the soldier to the stranger.

The young man, from all appearances not averse to his assignment, without hesitation moves in to do as he is bidden. Falling into stride with Jesus, he carefully slides his hand under the rough vertical beam where it has already grazed Jesus' skin and gently lifts the cross onto his own shoulder. And then, having hardly missed a step, the two continue to walk toward a distant hillock where Roman executions take place, known locally as the Skull Hill.

Far behind them from back near the Roman compound two more men, each also bearing a cross on his back, soon come into view. There are no more than a handful of soldiers to spur these on their way. Nor is there a crowd along the roadside to mark them, either with tears or taunts, in their death marches.

It is now nearly the ninth hour of the day. Thomas moves along a route parallel to the pathway at about the same distance as earlier but is keeping pace with the rest of the procession when the Skull Hill comes into view. He looks below and sees a few faces he recognizes, all of them the faces of women—Mary the Magdalene, another Mary, and Jesus' own mother come from Galilee. There are no men in their company, not a single disciple. Matthew, closest discile to the scene by five or six paces but still a safe way away, also moves with the crowd.

Soon, breaking through the Roman guard, goes Jesus' mother. She is weeping without letup as she darts toward her son. A soldier quickly intervenes to prevent her from reaching him.

She briefly struggles with him.

"He's my son! My son!" she pleads, but to no avail.

Another soldier moves in to help his comrade force her back. Thereupon John, from some distance back, rushes through spectators and soldiers to put his arm around her shoulders, in part apparently to prop her up lest she fall and in part simply to comfort her in her heartache. She turns to look up at him. Thomas, from a ways back, can see the woman's face. He sees in her eyes and in the lines of her face not only grief but horror. The woman is terrified.

The Twin thereupon scampers down the embankment to Matthew's side. "We're still far away," he tells him. "His kingdom may yet come."

"My son!" in the meantime Mary cries out, "Would to God I could die instead of you! My son, my son!"

"Possible but not likely," Matthew says. "I think he's resigned himself to this. He has to see it, for reasons we cannot begin to guess, as inevitable. Would he endure his own mother's broken heart if he felt at liberty to spare it? I think not."

"I don't understand."

"No one here understands, least of all her."

"Why doesn't he do something? Anything?" Thomas asks, trying not to sound utterly frantic, which he is. "He commanded a tempest at sea to be calm and, before you could blink an eye, it became a sea of glass. Nary a ripple as far as you could see. He commanded Lazarus to rise up out of his grave and he did. Cannot he not now hurl that cross so far into the winds that it will disappear somewhere beyond the Jordan? He can, Matthew! You know he can!"

"I do know he can. And if he chooses to do so, he'll have all Israel at his feet before the sun fades in the west. And no doubt a battalion of Romans as well."

"But you don't think that's about to happen."

"I think he's planning to ride this out, Thomas. Back in the Garden of Gethsemane Peter, they say, drew his sword against the arresting party, and Jesus told him to put it back. He wasn't about to put up fight or have anyone else do it in his behalf. You were at his trials. He said nothing in his defense, refuted no lie—and there were tons of them. Just let it happen. The best man we've ever known, the wisest and most lucid, the most godly, for some reason is about to let himself be crucified. And there is nothing he will do or apparently wants us to do to save him"

"It doesn't make sense!"

"But it is happening."

"Why? Will you tell me why? What earthly reason can there be?"

"I do not know! You sometimes make virtue of ignorance, Thomas. In this I am as fully virtuous as you. I know absolutely nothing."

"You think he wants to do it?"

"How could he possibly? But I do think he thinks he has to, if that's what you mean. He was sweating blood over it in the garden they said but finally threw up his arms as if it just had to be."

"Is this in the prophecies?" Thomas does not try to hide the edge in his voice.

"Something in Isaiah to that effect maybe—don't know. Does it matter?"

"A flicker of hope and, bang, a cloud of despair—somebody has one brutal sense of humor. You think he knew whatever you say it was in Isaiah?"

"He told us, didn't he? We just didn't listen. Hardly his fault."

"Then this is going to happen? His Father, our Father, is giving his nod? So it's all over: this dream, this wonderful fantasy of a kingdom of God on earth where the mighty will fall and the wretched and dispossessed will rise up to take their places, where a new vision of God Himself will light the way and the lamb will lie down with the lion and goodness and mercy will follow us all the days of our lives. The Christ who taught us love and hope will be killed for no reason at all, and we, rudely awaking from our dream, will scatter like so much dust in the whirlwind."

"There has to be some reason in this."

"Oblique at best," snaps Thomas, "none that I can see."

"I for one need to believe there is."

"You told me once that, when you didn't understand something, you were comforted by the idea that your father did and, when you realized he didn't, you found comfort in the thought the rabbi did and, when you realized he didn't either, then you were comforted by the illusion that the theologians surely did and, when you realized they were just full of themselves, you despaired of anyone's knowing anything—until Jesus came along, and then you found comfort again from that time on. Remember?"

"The story of my life. Of course, I remember."

"Well, that has been the story of my life as well. So tell me, where do we look now?"

Levi Matthew has no ready answer.

They are now closer to the sidelines en route to the Hill of the

Skulls. Thomas can almost reach out and touch John, who clutches Jesus' mother tightly against himself as they proceed on the heels of the dark-skinned stranger helping their master carry his cross. The other women from Galilee soon close about them. None of them speaks. Nor any longer do Thomas or Matthew. The moment is too awful for words.

There is already a circle of people being held at bay by soldiers at the crest of the hill where the executions are to take place and where, no doubt, the holes for the crosses have already been dug. Mary continues to weep, heaving as she does so. She is beyond consoling.

They ascend the slope, not a steep grade at all by the standards of the other hillocks about them but sufficiently steep to alter the pace of men under the weight of their crosses. There is loose gravel here that can send them quickly sprawling if they don't watch every step. People line either side of the path, the lead soldiers forcing them farther and farther away as they get closer to the crest.

Once atop the hill, even from the fringes they can see clearly what's there.

There are settled mounds of dirt with sprigs of grass growing on them marking the holes where the crosses are to be set. No fresh-dug dirt anywhere. The Romans apparently found it pointless to fill in holes that would be needed time and time again. There are bones lying about as well, not many but some, to remind people that what is not taken down and buried will quickly become feasted upon by vultures and crows and other scavengers. And next to the bones are shreds of clothing the carrion-eaters elected to pass up. And one can imagine, though none is visible, a skull or two hiding in the tall grass to the side—hence the name of the place.

The centurion presiding over the execution orders the stranger carrying Jesus' cross to advance to the vicinity of the holes and, with his thanks, tells him to lay down his burden there. When the other two condemned men arrive at the site only minutes later, he likewise instructs them to place their crosses on the ground beside the holes. There is nothing in voice or demeanor that suggests the centurion in anyway relishes his assignment. It's what he does. He's simply following orders.

All three men are offered wine mixed with drugs to deaden their pain before being nailed to their respective crosses. Jesus, after tasting this, refuses it. Immediately then he is ordered to lie down upon the longer beam of his cross so that his feet rest on a block secured to the shaft up a ways from its base, and his arms are stretched out along the shorter crosspiece. Three Roman soldiers thereupon commence to drive spikes with heavy iron mallets through his hands and feet and deep into the wood of the cross. The earsplitting, spirit-riving reports of metal striking metal echo throughout the region; they wash off the cliffsides and nearby hills to flood the valleys thereabouts with grim confirmation that a man and the hope he once embodied are both on the brink of nothingness.

Mary hears it and, wincing at every clang, buries her head yet deeper into John's chest. Thomas sees others of their ranks now. They, as he, are weeping copiously, writhing in their horror and grief—great drops of tears for their lord and doubtless, if they are like him, for themselves as well. Levi Matthew beside him is convulsing. Peter and Andrew near the edge of the crowd at the Skull Hill's approach are propping each other up lest their grief takes them to the ground.

To Thomas the clanging of the hammers is the knell that heralds the death of joy and the rebirth of unrelenting gloom. And, worse yet, the final abdication of God. It repudiates all that Jesus has said. It converts the very idea that God is Father into cruel fiction, for in this death is also the death of God, the beneficent Heavenly Father whom Jesus, with luster in his eyes and a lilt in his voice, continually talked about. "I am the truth," he told them just hours ago. The only lingering truth now is the incomprehensibly hideous one being told by the cacophonous clanging of hammers—the truth that nullifies all other truths.

He feels Levi Matthew, leaning into him, trembling as waves of shock course through his body when he hears the clanging too. It has to bring to his mind the euphoria that seemed to sweep over him the night Jesus ate at his table and he was first stricken by the notion that he was entertaining the Christ of God. That notion now has to be, bit by bit, beaten thin by the awful hammers.

If Jesus is not the Christ, good Levi, there never ever will be one. Never.

He thinks of Jesus' other disciples, some also on the edges of the assemblage, others farther away. They too must be hearing the clanging of the hammers and in empathy feel the iron spikes penetrate their own hands and feet. Shocks of pain have to be tearing at their bodies too, their hearts also broken by their master's agony, their spirits utterly crushed by the prospects of the inevitable. Sorrow, horror, rage, fear, despondency, dread —and hate too, it must be said, despite Jesus' clear teaching at that point—must be tearing at their souls.

The clanging of the hammers, the awful clanging of the hammers!

Weeping softly all the while, Mary in John's arms now suddenly wails loudly with all her might. Thomas sees John press her more tightly to himself, but she is beyond comforting. Tears gush down either cheek. Of all the hearts torn at the Skull Hill that hour, hers has to be torn the most, for she alone is weeping for her son.

The Roman soldiers waste little time once the spikes are driven home. They quickly hoist the three crosses bearing the three condemned men to upright positions and lower their bases down into the gaping holes nearby. Then, having already stripped all three of their robes, they bide their time at the foot of the crosses rolling dice to see who takes home the spoils of their morning's employment.

The crowd is not entirely one that has come to grieve. Two men, at the very moment the Roman soldiers set Jesus' cross in the ground, rush in to protest a placard that, at Pilate's insistence, has been nailed above his head, declaring in three languages that the victim is **King of the Jews**.

"Not true! Not true!" they cry. "It should read he said he was our king, not that he was!"

Five soldiers quickly corral them and force them back into the crowd, where they continue to shout their objections. When it is clear no one is listening they soon give up and resort to taunting.

There is a whole cadre of taunters. Thomas recognizes a number of them. Theirs are the same faces he saw at Jesus' trial: those of snarling, ranting, raucous men who came forward to give false testimony, those of perjurers who time after time swore they saw things that never happened and heard words never spoken. Theirs were the voices at Pilate's residence, the loudest and most strident in calling for Jesus' crucifixion.

There was always something about them he could not readily identify. Now he thinks he knows. They were too spontaneous, too precise in what they claimed Jesus said and did—and, for that matter, too outraged and angry. They had to have been put up to it, maybe rehearsed or coached. Hirelings told to mingle with the crowd and told exactly what to say and what emotions to ape. Paid out of the Temple treasury? Probably. The widow's mite put to foul use.

From their scattered places in the ranks of the onlookers, these men take turns railing against Jesus. The same edges are in their voices, the same histrionics in their gesticulations, and the same themes in their tirades as earlier that morning. But now, probably because it is a more open space, everything is pitched a notch higher. Raging, sneering, jeering, they hurl their jibes at Jesus.

"Savior of Israel, save yourself!"

"You were going to pull down the Temple and build it up again in three days. Why don't you save yourself?"

"Save yourself!"

"Save yourself!"

"Step on down, magician! Tear yourself loose and step on down from that cross!"

"Yes, step on down!"

"Great physician, heal yourself! Then we'll believe! Heal yourself and we will all believe!"

And so the first hours of Jesus' crucifixion pass. At one point the felon on Jesus' left twists himself so as to face the Galilean and joins in the heckling by pleading, with much more feeling than the play-actors in the crowd, "Oh, if you are the Christ, do come down from your cross—and take us down with you."

It is shortly after this that the tormentors, perhaps because they're growing hoarse—but more likely, Thomas concludes, because the term of their employment has terminated—give up their sport and singly begin to retreat from their various places in the crowd and then with no apparent emotion, like workmen from their fields of labor, quietly depart from the scene altogether. By shortly after midday the hostile element among the spectators has all but disappeared.

The sun is now enshrouded by clouds but is still dimly visible, though not for long. The Skull Hill now belongs to its three victims and the Roman soldiers overseeing their slow deaths— these and the grief-stricken, that horrified collection of Jesus' friends and family from Galilee.

Neither Jesus' mother nor Mary the Magdalene has ceased from weeping in all the time they have been there. Both women penetrate to within a few paces from Jesus' cross. The Magdalene seems loath to look up at Jesus, more loath to look anywhere else, unable to tear her eyes from him in his death throes, unable to endure what she sees.

She appears to be totally baffled by what she is witnessing.

Thomas understands. He knows exactly what she's thinking:

Others he has soothed and comforted, others he has saved even from death. Why then can he not save himself? Why doesn't he? There's no doubt but that he can. So why doesn't he? Did he choose this? Why, without protest, without struggle, does he submit himself to death and especially such a hideous death as this?

He can see that she wants desperately to do something for him. She aches maybe to wipe the grime and blood and sweat from his forehead with a cool, damp cloth and to clean the spittle from his cheeks and bathe his wounds with wine. The soldiers, however, as though protecting her from some foul contagion, interpose themselves every time she tries to get any closer and force her back.

Jesus' mother, now standing next to the Magdalene, is equally as frantic to tend to Jesus in his anguish, to take him into her arms the way she probably once did when he was a child and hurt himself at play or in working alongside his father. She's his mother. Why then will they not let her go to him?

"My son, my son," she protests to the soldiers softly.

But they do not seem to understand what she is saying and continue to keep her at bay, but Jesus from his cross does take notice. Thomas sees him as he looks down straight into his mother's eyes and then at John, whose arm is still around Mary's shoulders, and then back again at her and says weakly, though loud enough for all to hear, "From now on this man will be your son." And, his eyes back to his disciple, he says, "She will be your mother."

Shortly after this Jesus speaks again.

"I thirst," he says, his voice yet more feeble, but the soldiers understand and soak a sponge in vinegar, stick the sponge on the tip of a spear, and lift it up to his lips. He takes it into his mouth to suck on it for but a moment and then pushes it out with his tongue.

It is now mid-afternoon. The two men on either side of Jesus have long since slumped on their respective crosses, their heads bending downward so that their jaws are resting on their chests. There is no motion from either. Their legs, straight and rigid throughout the morning supporting most of their weight, have gone limp. Thomas judges that both are probably dead.

But Jesus is not. There are still indications of life in his face as well as his limbs. With obvious effort he raises his head and fixes his gaze upward. Then with a loud, trembling voice, as though trying to reach the ears of someone a great distance away, someone who might not even be there, he shrieks out, "My God! My God! Why have you forsaken me?"

With that he too commences to slump lifeless upon his cross. His lips open to say softly one more thing, but it is too faint for Thomas to pick up what it is. John and Mary, Jesus' mother, together with Mary the Magdalene and the other women from Galilee and some also from Judea, are standing now at the foot of Jesus' cross. Perhaps they made out those last words. He does not know.

Scattered about but positioned to see what is happening are Jesus' other ten disciples. They, as he, react with horror but also with relief when Jesus' body finally goes limp. At least his suffering is over.

Revelation

IT IS THE Sabbath. They drift in singly, one at a time, throughout the morning. Levi Matthew first. He is there when Thomas sidles in. Then the four fishermen almost on each others' heels though not quite. The metropolitans, Simon the Zealot, Thaddeus, the other James, and finally, after more than an hour, the other Judas. It is not to the Temple they come, not to the synagogue, but to the upstairs room where two days ago, a thousand years ago, a lifetime, Jesus washed their feet and sat down with them to eat the Passover supper. Judas Iscariot, having hanged himself during Jesus' crucifixion, is, of course, not there.

No one speaks. They barely acknowledge each other's presence. Each man to himself. Visages, carriages say all there is to say. All are stunned, broken, totally crushed by the events of the day before. Time and again one man or another will turn his head to the side to hide his face from the rest. No one says anything. Words intrude upon thoughts, even if words can be found, which they cannot be. Off and on Thomas hears someone trying to stifle tears and, once in a while, another given to very audible weeping. He stiffens, resolved not to do the same. When the greatest of men and the greatest of visions are swept beyond the pale, silence is the only eloquence, presence and proximity the only balms that will begin the healing. He would have wanted them there.

Thomas, seated in the chair he occupied that night, has pulled it back away from the table a cubit or so to underscore his wanting to be left alone. He does intermittently lift his head to glimpse those about him, careful to avoid eye contact, as others do the same. Everyone is seated where he was the night Jesus was betrayed. The four fishermen are in the middlemost. He wonders if maybe they might eventually wander back up to Galilee to rejoin their fishing fleets on Lake Gennesaret.

The Zealot could look up his old conspiracy comrades, but not likely. Any dreams the young fellow once entertained have probably been kicked out of him by this time. Fishing might fit him too. Levi Matthew will not be returning to this tax booth. That's for sure.

The kingdom they expected and the one Jesus talked about turned out to be two different things. That's what it all comes down to, and they should have picked up on that toward the end. There was never going to be an overthrow of the Jewish establishment, less so of the Roman command. Not by military might or popular uprising. Thomas sees that now. He hasn't figured out what Jesus' kingdom would have been, just that it would never have been what they initially thought it would. They were too literal. They didn't hear what he was saying. But the bits and pieces were there all the time. They would just have to try to put them together—later on maybe.

But not today. Though he is gone, today is his.

Thomas thinks his separate thoughts; the others think theirs. Each is calling up moments that most knocked him personally off-kilter, the things that most got his head spinning: Jesus' quieting a storm out on Gennesaret or his recitations of paradoxes up on the mountain or maybe his raising of Lazarus. How Thomas wishes he could hear his voice once more as it had been early on, like the voice of an angel, mellow and mesmerizing with an air of authority! See him smile that smile of his and hear him laugh his contagious laugh! See his heart go out to people in misery and sadness.

Not a man in the chamber is thinking of himself. Thomas can tell by their faces. None is pondering whether he may be next, fearing that perhaps Caiaphas and his minions might demand that they shoulder crosses too and be herded to the crest of the Skull Hill or that the Romans, fearing wholesale revolt, might initiate such action on their own. No such thoughts enter their minds at all. Grief alone consumes them.

They take their leaves the way they came, singly, one at a time. This after considerable time together. In almost the same order as when they arrived they make their exits: Matthew first, the fishermen, a couple others, the Zealot, somebody else, another and another, and finally the other Judas. Thomas lingers after his fellows have left, not a soul, not a sound anywhere about—the story of his life now. Jesus' last words, in his death throes gasped rather than spoken, "My God, my God, why have you forsaken me?" echo and reecho in his mind.

He does not know the answer to that cry.

There is no pact between the men as to when they will get together again or where. There is a bond, however, he knows, that binds them each to each. That they seem to know, though no words to that effect have been exchanged. A bond as strong as that of brothers. What also is left unsaid is that there are issues to be worked out before they do talk, issues each man alone has to come to terms with before they corporately go about trying to make sense of anything before they go on, if indeed they are going to go on at all.

Something has given beneath their feet. They have been walking along on hard, firm, even ground, and then something has shifted. Suddenly the gravel under their sandals is loose; the pathway begins to slope, gradually at first then precipitously. Bereavement such as they have never known is at the core of it. That they know. But there is more, there has to be more, and that is what they have to get straight in their collective minds.

Jesus once asked Thomas to what or whom he would compare him, and he responded, "No one. You are like no one or nothing I've ever known."

And two mornings ago in Annas's courtyard, they say, Peter blurted out to the girl near the fire where he was warming himself, "I don't know him."

Thomas, having learned of Peter's denial, wonders now if there was not truth in both their declarations. The man was certainly enigmatic if anything. Even prophecies about the Christ were shrouded in mystery, when one thinks about it—also paradoxical at points. He has now identified the passage from Isaiah that Matthew alluded to: Out of one side of his mouth the great prophet proclaimed the coming of the Lord of lords and the King of kings, the Everlasting

Father, the Prince of Peace; then out of the other side he gave posterity the image of a scourged, beaten, and mangled martyr. A human scapegoat as it were. What did they miss that apparently Isaiah did not?

Matthew, who knew the Scriptures better than anybody else, should have seen the paradox all along. Why did he not say something? He knew the Christ was to be born in Judea. How could he have possibly overlooked his whole prophetic profile? Thomas will have to delve further the next time he sees him. Yes.

But the problem is that he may never see Matthew again.

The men will, of course, meet again tomorrow as they did today; however Thomas will not be in their midst. No meeting has been called, but they will be there. It's simply in them to do that. Today was to share their common sorrow and confirm that what happened indeed did happen, then to recognize that he was dead and wasn't going to be there for them anymore and, as painful as it was, they had to get used to it, to make whatever adjustments they had to and somehow be there for each other. The first stage of grief. Silence befitted the occasion. Nothing could have been said to make it less unbearable.

But tomorrow they will talk—talk about him, the times they had, the things he said, the wonders he performed, what might have been but now will never be. They will try to smile through tears and will chatter on top of each other. And they will mean well.

He will not be there though.

More than going some place he wants to go, he will be leaving a scene he needs to leave; for he cannot be in the upstairs room when the other ten convene there that next day. He knows too well how it will go. They'll talk then, talk enough to atone for their silence of today; they will comfort themselves with memories of their times with Jesus, fancying how life would be if he were still with them. They'll wonder what he'd have them do now that he was dead and then soon will be contemplating new fancies. They'll construct scenarios for the kingdom that did not come and now never will.

These are precisely the things Thomas wishes to escape.

The emotions will themselves be more than he can bear, and the pointless prattle will reduce the substance of the most overshadowing event of their collective lives into little more than an exercise to get over it. He does not want to get over anything—least of all endure an assault on his very soul.

There is nothing ahead any more. He ponders the life he once knew, the life he'd turned his back on three years ago to follow the mysterious Nazarene he took to be the Christ and, curiously, still does. That life now seems shoddy and empty. He dreads the prospect of facing anything without Jesus.

He is, however, logical and realistic. Oh yes, his memories of Jesus are good, and it would be magnificent to have him back. He knows that, but the man's dead. Idle conversations with the others would only make his grief the more unbearable. He's dead! That's the overriding fact, hideous and painful, but nevertheless there. All a man can do is accept it and be on his way.

He leaves the upper room to find the nearest gate that will take him out of the city to be on his way. Where he knows not, not even the direction. Just away. Not to think about any one thing in particular, but everything in general as if to untangle threads connecting one thing to another. Not an act of self-pity but one of rational quest—not even of choice but of compelling necessity.

And so he wanders, first westerly toward an unpopulated region. Path leads to path, and soon he has no idea where he is. Irrelevant anyway. Into the night he wanders, now and probably for the rest of his life, set adrift with neither pilot nor star to guide his way. When, because of the blackness about him, he can no longer pick his way, he sits down at path's edge and quickly falls into a dreamless sleep. He awakens to dawn's first light and is soon on his way again.

He wonders when Jesus first knew his own fate. When he first spoke of it cryptically to them or way back before he even called them? Or maybe when he was twelve and, according to his mother, confounded the theologians at the Temple with his knowledge and insight? Yes, it could have been that early. Could he have known then that he would be crucified before his kingdom came, before he had somehow managed to save his people? If so, what were the three years all about when he was leading them?

Jesus was a man of reason. Time and time again he demonstrated that much in his run-ins with the Pharisees. Leagues ahead of them logically every single time. Everything he said had the ring of truth in it. The most lucid mind by far Thomas has ever encountered. You knew that whatever Jesus said was true but also had the distinct feeling that beyond those truths were other truths alluded to but not spelled out, that there were mysteries he was not about to divulge. Things that simply could not be grasped and so could not be comprehended in language. The man had the power of God in his fingertips all right and the thoughts of God upon his lips, yet neither touch nor word to spare himself. He had to be the Christ. Who else could he have been?

But at some point he knew for a fact he was going to be crucified. He out and out knew it! How does that figure? What was the reason then behind the three-year Odyssey that ended on the Skull Hill? What was the sense of any of it, if it had to end that way? Does sense make sense, and does reason even enter into the equation? If the Christ was crucified, was there such a thing as justice in the world at all? Or sense for that matter either?

That was Job's big complaint. He protested that God was unjust— such was the gist of it anyway. And God spoke to him out of the whirlwind, saying that he had no standing to call Him into question and that was that.

But Jesus did the same, did he not? He said, "My God, my God, why have you forsaken me?" Wasn't that calling God into question too? Could it be that Jesus did have standing where Job did not? Was his question merely about himself, or was it generic? Could it have been for all of them?

And so Thomas trudges on, weary in his bones, wearier yet in his soul; hunger gnawing at his stomach unheeded and unattended—his famished mind feeding on fluff, pangs unabated. On, on he goes in this direction and that, ever drawn into wildernesses of one kind or another. All that day he wanders without thought of where he is or where he is going.

It is late in the afternoon when he finally once more comes upon familiar paths, and these lead back toward the Holy City rather than away from it. Deferring his aimless journey to another day, he continues on to the quarters where he has been staying for the past week and by nighttime is settled back in.

It is there early the follow morning that, shaking off a nightmarish dream, he becomes aware of someone's opening the door of the room where he is lying atop a pallet. He turns in place and sees the kindest face he's ever known, that of Levi Matthew. The man is angelic with excitement.

"He's alive!" Matthew sings out right away. With his closest friend are the other nine in an arc around him, men no longer in mourning, their faces all as beatific as Levi's.

"It's true!" blares Peter, speaking for all of them. "The Magdalene and some of the women yesterday morning, at just after dawn, went to the garden where he was entombed in a man-made cave, which the Romans had secured with a huge boulder. They'd even posted guards to make sure nobody could steal his body away. Well, when the women got there they found the stone rolled away and the guards stunned as though dead. That's when they came on a run to us."

"Then what?"

"The Magdalene said, 'Somebody's taken the body of Jesus, and we don't know where they've laid him.' We raced there as fast as we could. John got there first and got down and looked into the sepulcher."

"And, as she said, it was empty," John spiritedly comes in. "There was enough light so I could tell."

"Then, when I got there," Peter, voice constant, picks up the narrative, "I plowed straight in all the way. His burial linens were there and in another place the cloth they'd put over his face, neatly rolled up, but there was no body. Someone had taken him."

"Certainly none of us," says Andrew, excitement in his voice too.

"Nor does it seem like the Romans," Peter goes on. "What would be the point?"

"There'd be no reason for the Temple crowd either," the Zealot now says. "Got what they were after. If anything, you'd think they'd want him completely forgotten, and the sooner the better."

"And so for an hour or more we confronted the mystery of the missing body," continues Peter. "So who did it, we wondered, and why? Friend or foe? Was somebody out to perpetrate new outrages on his corpse and, if so, to what end?"

The Zealot steps toward Thomas. "I thought it was maybe some insurgent group, my old pals maybe or the Sicarii."

"And then the most amazing thing happened!" says Peter, taking charge again.

"What amazing thing was that?"

"We were all standing around, nobody knowing what to do, where to start looking, and suddenly, as if we were all frozen on the spot, there is total hush in the room. No one in motion, not a soul breathing. We were like statues, totally stiff. All our eyes were fixed on a figure standing near the door. It was Jesus, and he began to step slowly into our midst. 'Peace, dear friends, peace upon you,' came a familiar voice."

"Breath still suspended, we were hesitant to respond," Levi Matthew then tells Thomas.

Peter picks up the narrative again. "Then he said as buoyantly, and maybe more so, as he did the first time, 'Peace upon you all! The Father sent me. And thus I in turn am sending you. Here, I breathe upon you now the Spirit of God.' So saying, he brought his hands to his mouth, like so, and literally, as if blowing chaff from his palms or whiffing out a candle, he exhaled a long breath over us.

"We moved back as he advanced, giving him wide berth, but were all close enough him to see the gashes in his hands and feet made by the spikes and the smaller wounds made by the thorns along his brow. He seemed very, very glad to see us all again and totally impervious to the marks of brutality on his own body. He was wearing an old robe, so the tear in his side by the soldier's lance did not show. No one reached out to touch him, nor did he invite any of us to do so. Retreating as he came, he soon exited the chamber."

Quickly others jump into the conversation, then all at once, talking on top of each other, each getting in his own take, in broad agreement but all citing details that most caught their own attentions. Their voices tempered from their earlier bursts of thunder to merest cacophony, to a man they exhibit uninhibited excitement the likes of which Thomas has never quite encountered in his adult years. There's an animation in their voices and gestures he has not witnessed in a very long time. He abides them at first, then throws up his arms and at the top of his own voice shouts out for them to stop.

"You're all mad!" he tells them. "You're mad, mad, mad!"

"We saw him!" insists Matthew, in closer to him. "Mary the Magdalene saw him too in the garden where he was buried. She talked with him."

Thomas holds out his hand to keep his friend at bay. "Then the madness has become contagious. He died. We all saw him die. The Roman drove his spear into his side. Remember? The man's dead. You're seeing apparitions."

"Not so!" says Peter, also stepping toward him. "He's alive, believe me, Thomas! And he came to us and he spoke to us."

"Thirst-filled men in the desert see water at every rise. The deeply bereaved see their beloved departed in every doorway and every bend of the road. Desperate people see what they need to see. It happens. I understand, I do. And that's exactly what's happening to you right now."

"We saw him!" they all shout at once.

"Stop! Stop! This I cannot bear!"

"Grieve no more, dear Thomas," Matthew tells him. "He has risen. We're all witnesses to that. We've seen him with our own eyes and heard him with our own ears. You have to believe us. What we're telling you is as true as our standing before you now."

"Believe! Believe!" others begin to chime in.

This is more than Thomas can take. As they speak, he can feel his heart beating faster, his pulse quicken, and his skin grow hot with emotion. Spikes are being driven through his own hands and feet. He can almost feel them. He heaves mightily as though suffocating.

"I will not believe! Except I myself see in his hands the marks of the nails and stick my finger into them," he screams at the top of his voice, "and drive my hand into his side, I will not believe!"

His words, he realizes, are cruel to those who mourn Jesus. They certainly must bring back the image of his death. But somehow he has to make his position clear—irrevocably clear.

They press him no more. And soon he runs from the room as though from ghosts.

After a whole week passes and nothing happens, Thomas, with no other place to go, slinks back to the upper room to see if his fellow disciples might still be holed up in their safe house. They are. Peter opens the door to his knock and then closes and bolts it again after he quickly slips in. They rarely go out, he quickly discovers, except to procure food and other necessaries, making sure that the door remains locked and at night also barred.

He finds the ten men are jubilant and filled with anticipation. The topic of Jesus' purported return to life does not at first enter their conversation. Apparently a silent pact exists between them about what to talk about openly, should he return, and what not to. Thomas silently and somberly bides his time. He is not about to bring up the matter himself. Even though all Jerusalem is abuzz with speculations about the mysterious disappearance of the great Galilean's body, he allows his fellows leave to enjoy their collective illusion. It keeps them happy for the time being, and that is fine with him.

The official explanation in Jerusalem for the happenstance, he already knows, is that some of Jesus' more zealous followers sneaked up on the soldiers guarding the sepulcher and knocked them unconscious—either that or someone was able to lace their wine with some potion or other to effect the same end. That would have given them more than sufficient time to chisel away the sealant and roll back the stone to whisk the corpse away. The word on the street is that the guards were bribed and thus were themselves party to the ruse. They might even have helped with the boulder.

Thomas himself does not know what to think. Unless Jesus had another corps of disciples he never knew about, neither theory seems plausible. Chicanery is the last thing anyone associated with the Nazarene would ever resort to. Trickery, deceit, hoax, fabrication, bribery—no, never! He eyes each of his fellow disciples closely. Certainly none of them! But if not, then who?

It is now day eight after the disappearance of Jesus' body, and with Thomas's return all eleven disciples are now in the room. Earlier that morning two of them went out briefly to procure food at the market, but they came back just prior to Thomas's entrance and apparently were explaining the community's latest theory of the missing corpse when he knocked. The conversation now quickly shifts to the practical matter of what provisions they had in store and what they would soon have to restock. The transition is not a smooth one; the men stumble to make it seem like an issue of importance.

"It's okay," Thomas finally assures them. "Speak as you will."

"Apparently there's a new theory out there," says Levi Matthew.

"Yes," explains Simon the Zealot, one of the men who had been to the market, "a third explanation seems to have surfaced: that Jesus was not dead after all and he revived once inside the sepulcher and pushed back the boulder himself, overpowering the guards as well, to make his escape."

"Sounds like nonsense," Matthew retorts.

"Closer than the rest of the explanations—I'll say that much," offers Peter, "but still wide of the mark."

"If they only knew," says the Zealot

Thomas holds his piece. His soul burns within him, but he knows that, by opening the door, he's already said enough. Probably too much, he allows. Let them have their illusions for now, he thinks, for sooner or later they will, as he already has, have to come to terms with reality.

Already standing apart from the others, he steps yet further back and turns his head away. If they're going to return to their favorite theme, he still wants them to know it's okay with him. He simply does not want to participate in it. He keeps his head low as if deep in thought. Then slowly he lifts his eyes.

And soundlessly, suddenly, there he is! Jesus, stripped of outer robe, standing among them! What every sense within Thomas declares cannot be in an instant is; what cannot possibly be appears, not a specter but in the flesh before him.

There is no doubt it is he. If nothing else, the marks in the figure's hands and the long cut in his side identify him. He passes by the others and heads straight for Thomas. The eyes of the man called Twin follow his every move. Within him shock mingles with shame.

Jesus, advancing, stares directly at him.

"Thomas," he says, stretching forth his hands, "reach out your finger and feel my hand." Then, before Thomas can answer, Jesus closes the distance between them and turns to expose, full on, his ugly side wound. "Reach out your hand and thrust it in there, if you will. Do, dear Thomas. Doubt no longer. Believe!"

The disciple gasps and shrinks from this awful invitation. Frantic and awestricken, he gazes first at Jesus' hands and then his side. A thousand thoughts now explode in Thomas's mind, a thousand scales fall at once from his eyes. In an instant a thousand images of Jesus, his words and actions, rush into his consciousness and begin to take on focus.

This man before him is more than a man. But what? he wonders. Who . . . just who is he? The briefest of instances passes, and the pieces suddenly fall into place. The picture is complete, and an impulse tells him who Jesus really is.

Slowly Thomas raises his eyes to Jesus' and, sinking to his knees before him, cries, "My Lord and my God!"

CPSIA information can be obtained at www.ICGtesting.com
Printed in the USA
BVOW08s0215280114

343127BV00003B/27/P